"Jonathan Carey offers to pastors and laymen alike a clear-cut directive on how to bring into focus your God-given vision. There is no doubt today that many are carrying around a vision along with a desire to 'see it happen' but with no idea how to bring it about. I highly recommend this book to all pastors and leaders. When we cease to have a vision, we die. An active vision brings life and joy into lives. We accomplish God's best by having a well-articulated vision. This material will help you to formulate your vision and ministry. My only regret is that I did not have this book and workbook when I began my ministry forty-two years ago. I am challenged once again to give my all to the vision that God has set before me."

Ernest M. DeLoach
Veteran Pastor and Missionary

PRACTICAL WISDOM FOR

Building *your* Vision

THE PRACTICAL WISDOM SERIES

Jonathan Carey

PRACTICAL WISDOM FOR Building *your* Vision

Life Principles to Guide You

Tate Publishing & *Enterprises*

Published by Tate Publishing & Enterprises, LLC
127 E. Trade Center Terrace | Mustang, Oklahoma 73064 USA
1.888.361.9473 | www.tatepublishing.com

Tate Publishing is committed to excellence in the publishing industry. The company reflects the philosophy established by the founders, based on Psalms 68:11,
"The Lord gave the word and great was the company of those who published it."

Cover design by Steven Jeffrey
Interior design by Janae J. Glass

Published in the United States of America

ISBN: 978-1-60247-911-1
1. Christian Nonfiction: Church and Ministry 2. Pastoral Helps: Professional Growth

07.08.08

This book is dedicated to my spiritual mentor and friend,
Rev. Ernest M. DeLoach of Key West, Florida, USA.

Acknowledgments

I wish to thank my wife, Shena, for her invaluable input, support, and patience during this writing exercise. This book would have never been possible without her.

To my parents, Morton and Cora Carey, thank you for having provided the environment where dreams flourished and love was unconditional. I daily thank God for you both.

To the CTC Network Family in Freeport, Bahamas, thank you for providing the forum for these ideas and concepts to be presented and evaluated. This is really our accomplishment.

Table of Contents

Foreword

Vision is key to succeeding; after all, it is vision that enables us to see opportunities where others see only challenges, and that allows us to see victory where others see defeat. Vision reaches into the nothingness of the present circumstances to grab hold of a possibility that is not so apparent. One does not build pyramids, a great wall, a great company, or a great religion without vision. What is true in these big areas of life is also true in individual lives; vision is critical.

Practical Wisdom for Building Your Vision, by Rev. Jonathan Carey, is a work by someone who is uniquely insightful and practical. In this useful prose, Rev. Carey provides clear instructions for all to follow in building a vision for success in almost any area of life. Using powerful biblical references and practical illustrations of the process that leads to vision building, Rev. Carey provides for his readers a good guide for a meaningful achievement in life. Not only does he present the positive opportunities that vision building presents, he also speaks to the challenges that those seeking to do so must encounter and provides wisdom for overcoming those challenges.

This work will be useful to leaders in all kinds of organizations, be they church, business, school, or government. It will also be helpful for those simply seeking to gain a clearer focus in life. I recommend it to readers as a useful work by a truly gifted and insightful teacher.

The Hon. Zhivargo S. Laing
Minister of State for Finance
The Commonwealth of The Bahamas

Preface

The Way Forward

One cool Bahamian night while rain was dancing off window panes, two young brothers in the comfort of their home were feasting on cheese sandwiches and washing them down with glasses of cold milk. Unbeknown, their mother was observing from a distance and wondering in her heart what her sons would become as men.

When the opportunity presented itself, she inquired of them what they wished to do with their lives once they became grown. The older shared first, then the younger his dream. He said, "Mommy, I want to help people."

Thirty-five years later, the younger brother, now a preacher, is standing in front of a group of primary school students. Looking into their eager eyes, he thinks what possibilities may lay in the souls of these children. He shares a story with them of the *Triple D* to success: *Desire, Discipline, and Determination.* This all takes place in the one-room school building of a quiet fishing village on a remote island in the Caribbean and concludes in about one-half hour. The preacher has now completed the first phase of his routine when visiting a new community to hold revival meetings. The other phase is visiting the settlement's cemetery.

That evening prior to the first meeting and while the sun is sleepily setting, he respectfully walks through the cemetery, reading headstones, and wondering how many that peacefully lay had fulfilled their dreams. As he reflects on his own life, he inwardly hears the Holy Spirit ask, *What do you want to do with your life?* After a few thoughtful moments he responds, *I want to be in a position to help people.*

The preacher at that moment fully realizes that a vision without a mission and action steps is fruitless. He puts pen to paper there in the cemetery and writes a brief outline for the book you now hold in your hands.

I am that preacher, and it is my prayer that this book will add to the richness of your life and ministry.

What to Expect

Practical Wisdom for Building Your Vision is just that. It's a book that presents practical wisdom principles for leaders related to building their visions, organizations, ministries, and personal lives. God gives vision; however, we are partly responsible for its fulfillment. This book was written in an attempt to provide answers for various vision fulfillment challenges.

The format of the book is a four-part one and has a personal study section at the end of the first three sections. This format encourages personal interaction with the presented material and also allows for corporate evaluation, enrichment, and growth. The book may be used in small group settings, and I encourage you to complete each personal study section; this will reinforce the practical wisdom principles gleaned.

The first part of the book discusses what a vision is and offers ideas for its development, fulfillment, and promotion. Readers are given numerous illustrations and examples from the Word of God and the writer's life.

Part two focuses on the leader's personal life, discussing the need for understanding the purpose of life and the necessity for prayer, counsel, and faith. This section is intended for personal evaluation, enrichment, and growth. God builds the leader first and then the organization or ministry. Both experienced and inexperienced leaders will find this section enriching. It informs and reminds us of important Christian leadership attributes.

The third part of the book stresses the importance of organizational structures and how to identify vision shifts and challenges. This may be of great support to leadership teams in that it points out the need for clearly defined roles in an organization's foundational and operational structures. It is a brief section and stresses the need for an organization or ministry to understand its philosophy as it relates to vision casting.

The fourth and last part provides you with the building your vision 5RCircle of Success. This process was developed over a three-year span of field testing with Christian organizations and churches. It is designed to take you through the complete building of your vision process and leave you with a working blueprint for continued success. In short, the book provides from cover to cover practical wisdom principles and an opportunity for continued assistance through offered consultation and workshops. Let's begin the process!

A Clear Vision

Vision: Clear, Challenging, and Future Focused

"What could be worse than being blind?" was a question posed to the great leader Helen Keller, who was physically blind and deaf. She responded, "Having sight but no vision."[1]

> "Blessed are your eyes for they see."
> Matthew 13:16

> "Write the vision and make it plain upon tables, that he may run that readeth it. For the vision is yet for an appointed time; But at the end it shall speak, and not lie. Though it tarry, wait for it; because it will surely come, it will not tarry."
> Habakkuk 2:2, 3

It is important to have a vision. A vision conveys a focused direction to an organization's thrust and helps create and ensure the continuation of an idea, project, or goal. Equally important is the clarity of that vision. The vision should have 20/20 sight. A 20/20 vision *has discernment and short and long-range perspective in thinking.* For the reader, it is plain or evident; it is unmistakably clear.

Every vision must have a mission. The mission is a road map and a vehicle used by the vision for its success. Simply put, the mission is the main tool for accomplishing the vision. The mission contains the major areas of focus or goals, action steps for completion of stated goals, and a declaration or mission statement. *Here is an example of a vision producing a mission*:

- The vision of God the Father is the extension of the Kingdom of Heaven onto the earth through humanity.
- The Mission of Jesus Christ the Son as it relates to the vision is the proclamation and reintroduction of the Kingdom of Heaven on the earth.

We could continue developing this process by listing the mission statement, major areas, and action steps the Godhead uses to complete this vision.

> Throughout this book, you ought to interpret the reference to vision as: a vision complete with a mission statement, major areas of focus, and well-defined action steps. A complete vision is biblical, future oriented, directional, and functional.

A Clear Vision Influences

As a teenager, I was able to secure a few summer jobs. By far the most intriguing one was as a sales clerk in a camera shop. The shop was located on a famous shopping strip in The Bahamas, the world renowned Bay Street, in the city of Nassau, on the island of New Providence. The camera shop was a major attraction for American tourists in that our merchandize was marked below the USA suggested retail prices.

The hottest items outside of a camera and a Cuban cigar were camera filters. The camera lens, when fitted with a filter, would result in tinting the original lens color. A new, vision-friendly color would emerge.

Psychologically, we all see life through tinted lens; our filters are uniquely different. Personal and family experiences greatly influence our values and personalities; this, mixed with culture and training, help shape our thinking and recognition processes, and we become uniquely wired. Unfortunately, even though we are comfortable with our psychological filters, often they are faulty, and adjustments or removal altogether may be required. There may be dozens of shades of thinking in any one community. A *clear vision* helps remove some of the negative influences of those tints, presents common ground, and radiates a "God objective" purpose. A clear vision shines light into dark places.

The vision must be clear to the organization, the saved society that you serve, and the lost society that you hope to reach and serve. It must be clear to all possible stakeholders and target groups. Clarity increases the chances of understanding, acceptance, and support.

The Saved Society

The "saved society" consists of people who have made the spiritual decision to accept Jesus Christ as Savior and Lord. They are both the Christians belonging to and those not belonging to your particular organization. The saved society will naturally view the vision from a different perspective than unbelievers. They view it from a biblical vantage point. The vision presented to them must be clear, in that it reflects the heartbeat of God as revealed in the Scriptures.

The possible exposure to a broad segment of believers makes it important for your vision to reflect a Kingdom mindset as opposed to a local or nuclear church mindset. This is because many are not interested only in a local vision but also one that is universal in scope. The nuclear church vision is contained and interwoven in the Kingdom vision.

Jesus said to His disciples, "The Kingdom of God is within you" (Luke 17:21). God's Kingdom has no territorial or traditional boundaries. Wherever a group of people honor Jesus Christ as Savior and purpose to worship God, there is the Kingdom. The church is then extended.

When as an organization we launched a Sunday morning service called *Power Plus,* we were convinced that the Lord wanted us to teach leadership and empowerment principles to a selected core group. After the first year, there was amazing growth in our spiritual, personal, and professional lives. The principles and core values taught and displayed reshaped and redefined our lives.

The vision challenged us to a place of inward transformation. Are we a local church? Not in the traditional sense. I refer to us as a corporate or workplace ministry. Steadily, we are reaching a new core of individuals with this vision thrust. The physical plant is our corporate office in the city of Freeport on Grand Bahama Island in The Bahamas. This is one example of the church extended and is a growing expression in Christendom.

The Vision Has to Align Itself with the Kingdom Vision

The Kingdom vision consists of a mandate to reach people everywhere, transforming societies and transcending the local church's sphere of influence. It is a vision that includes church growth and church planting but is larger in scope. It is a vision, as summed up in a part of the Lord's Prayer, "Your Kingdom come. Your will be done on earth as it is in heaven" (Matthew 6:10). There are many in the Body of Christ that understand this mission of the Kingdom vision. (God's will is to be done on the earth, and the accomplishment of this mission is at the core of the Kingdom vision.) They are members of local churches but have also taken their place as members of the universal church and see themselves as a part of the thrust of the Kingdom of God on the earth. Present a vision that is unmistakably clear to them.

The Lost Society

The lost society is the group in your community and sphere of influence that is not Christian. Some may be churched, others unchurched and unaware of their spiritual condition. They will have a slightly different set of rules and perspectives than the saved society. The vision, to be clear to the lost society, must show how what you envision connects with them. It ought to be in a language that they readily understand and at a level that is not over their heads. Remember, you are projecting a Kingdom vision, a vision that welcomes workplace ministry.

Workplace Ministry

Workplace ministry is ministry that can and does take place almost anywhere and "among" any people group. The assembling of "church" almost anywhere is a *mindset that must be embraced and cultivated.* The world is our mission field. People are not beating a path toward the traditional church building or ministry; however, we have the responsibility of modeling Jesus Christ. This modeling takes place in the community and realms of society where we all live and work. The Kingdom vision promotes the church's social responsibility. Fulfilling our social responsibility is an aggressive approach and agenda. We must reach out to others in sincere and tangible ways. The church must take its place in bringing about social reform. God desires the transformation of communities and nations; He wants to influence all realms of society. He wants His message taken throughout the earth. We are not passive ambassadors. You want to communicate a vision that is export in its mentality. Meet them in their world and yours. Take "church" to them.

The presentation of a straightforward and clearly worded vision to all target groups will help produce the desired outcomes. A clear vision is a reflection of clear thinking. When I was a kid, there was a song that had this catchy stanza: "I can see clearly now the rain is gone, I can see all obstacles in my way."[2] That's the power of a clear vision.

In our quoted text (Habakkuk 2:2, 3), the prophet Habakkuk relays the reward of a clear vision as determined by God Himself. Here is its summation:

Readers will embrace a clear and plainly written vision, working toward its fulfillment. It is safe to conclude that an unclear vision will produce little positive effect, and, if at all, it will make small forward steps toward its realization. Uncertainty stifles activity. There will be no "running with it."

Here are four *Practical Wisdom* points that a clear vision will produce:

1. Paint a Picture
2. Remain Visible
3. Be Understood
4. Gain Influence

A Picture Paints a Thousand Words

As a young preacher, my pastor and mentor encouraged me to think in pictures as I prepared and then delivered sermons. Since I struggled with a speech impediment that would often manifest itself in the middle of a sentence, possible solutions were welcomed with hopeful enthusiasm. The intent was to get me to paint a mental picture of the message and then allow the Holy Spirit to help me use my vocabulary to articulate the message to the audience. To my amazement, the stuttering left, and the delivery of sermons became smooth and polished. The painting of a picture with words worked for me and is still a part of my preparation and delivery process. I find continuing value and comfort in this exercise. When God gives us a dream, is it not in picture form? Your vision ought to be a picture painted with words that others may see, understand, and be given an opportunity to support. A clearly painted vision has the potential to eliminate the stutters of life. Here are some *Practical Wisdom* points to consider:

1. It has been said that a person remembers more of what is seen than heard. If this is true, then more painting pictures with words should be the order of the day, and this technique may, over time, become as valuable as canvases, paints, and brushes.
2. It is effective to write the vision in a form that lends itself to the use of illustrations and graphs. Illustrations and graphs tend to paint vivid pictures. There are computer software packages on the market that will greatly assist with this.
3. It is also wise to secure constructive criticism on the vision's presentation and then make the necessary adjustments. These adjustments are mostly to the writing style and presentation of the content, not necessarily changing the content, but refining the style and delivery if and when necessary. I say constructive criticism as opposed to comments because you want to present the best possible picture of God's intent. So bite the bullet and view the criticism as intended. Conduct this exercise among different target groups and trusted friends.
4. Perhaps you can write a short, then medium, and lastly a long version of the vision. Practice sharing the vision and become comfortable with sharing each of the three lengths. I often share the vision with strangers in my travels and enjoy this immensely, especially on airplanes. In this setting, undivided attention is usually secured. Practice your God-given vision on others.

Keep the Vision Visible

Many organizations have developed vision statements and then file them away out of sight and reach. This is a grave mistake. The vision to be successful must be at the forefront and kept visible at all times and at any cost. As a rule, people are very forgetful and learn better through repetition. The vision statement ought to be placed in public areas, taught to members of the organization, and promoted throughout the community it wishes to reach and serve. Make it clear and always keep it visible.

In 1993, I was appointed by The Bahamian Government's Ministry of Education to develop an alternative public high school for at-risk students. During the six years of its development, I spoke to civic groups, churches, and wrote updates for the local newspaper. These were all in an effort to keep the school at the forefront. Many of the presentations at the civic organizations received media coverage. The message, as I thought, was being galvanized in the mind of the community. Surprisingly, even with these continuing efforts, almost daily someone would say they never heard of the institution. At the end of this exercise, it became apparent that it is virtually impossible to overpublicize. *Publicize*, *publicize*, *publicize*, and again I say *publicize*. Conduct a brainstorming session with your leadership team and list other creative ways to promote your God-given vision. Make thinking outside the box the *Practical Wisdom* ground rule.

It Must Be Clearly Understood

Often, leaders are guilty of writing or communicating in a way that is misunderstood or not understood at all. This greatly hinders the goal of the organization and alters the charted forward focus. When miscommunication occurs, leaders find themselves backtracking, mending fences, and soothing egos. Often, the positive influence sought after, which is mandatory for success, is potentially lost forever.

Influence is the art of winning people's cooperation. It involves shaping the way people feel and think about something. A clearly understood vision greatly enhances influence and provides additional opportunities for success. God-given ideas and good intentions will never come to fruition without the support of others. Miscommunication is one factor that will keep a vision in the realm of unfulfilled dreams.

Here are a few Practical Wisdom tips that may result in positive influence:

State the Common Ground

As you show your organization's vision, values, and goals, be careful to show also how they connect with those whom you are trying to reach. Present what you have in common. You will have to do your homework and properly understand your target group. See things from their perspective; be sympathetic with their needs and dreams; then show them how cooperating with you can help them achieve what they want. God gives us a vision, but that vision is always about improving the lives of others.

The vision must include how God addresses their needs and dreams. The vision should point them in the direction of God's mission for their lives, the community where they live, and the world of which they are a part. It has to connect to be effective. It has to be seen as mutually beneficial.

Care About the People You Want to Influence

People know when you care. They hear it in your voice, see it in your actions, and feel it in their hearts. If you show that you value them, they will eventually respond positively. They will, at one point or another, let their guards down and freely communicate. Perhaps you may want to also project a "go and do" attitude in the community as opposed to having a "come and see" one. Here is an example of caring and gaining influence. The Bahamas, as a family of islands, is always prone to hurricanes. Once after a devastating hurricane, I saw a group passing out water bottles, and their vision statement was labeled on the bottles. It left a visible, informative reminder of who cared enough to assist them in their plight. It is important to communicate your concern for your target group's welfare, safety, and development. Why not display your vision too? Vision statements on labels become pointers back to your organization. The style of your writing and the warmth of your presentation will also convey your compassion. Let me caution you here: God gives us compassion for others. As we stay connected to Him, we will move in this spirit of compassion. We must maintain the Heart of God in all our ministry endeavors.

Help People Believe Change Is Possible

People often know, although they seldom admit, that they need to change. Many feel trapped in an endless, vicious cycle and wonder if life will ever get better for them. Nevertheless, they persist in doing what they have always done. Thinking they are doing the best they can, they remain in their unproductive or underachieving cycle. Show them a better way, but more importantly, convince them that change is possible. Do not just give them a solution; offer them hope too. We must communicate hope. *The Holy Bible* contains numerous stories of hope—hope for individuals, families, communities, and nations. Remember the words of the apostle Paul, "That if we as believers do not have a hope beyond the grave we are then of all men most miserable" (1 Corinthians 15:19). Clearly show the connection between your vision and God's plan of redemption, empowerment, and hope.

Time Your Presentation Well

There is a time and a season for everything, especially for presenting a vision and asking for support. Pray earnestly before each presentation. Look for "moments of influence." Moments of influence are times when your target group is comfortable. Make your best presentation during these times.

As a young pastor in a small settlement, it was my custom to walk the community in the late afternoon, fellowshipping with the folks by entering into their chores. If someone was shelling peas or cleaning their property, I would offer to assist; this proved very successful. Often in these moments, I was allowed to share the gospel message and our vision for the community. Over time I became known as the community pastor and often would be called to the bedside of an ailing member of the community who never visited our local church. The church was now being extended and the power of influence seen. This was, in part, to "well-timed" presentations. Moments of influence are there; you have to have keen sight to perceive them and a willingness to incorporate them in your thinking process and plans. For pastors, baby dedications, weddings, and funerals are some other moments of influence. Make a list of ones that are applicable to your setting.

Use Correct Terminology for the Target Group

There is an organization in a North American inner city that is apostolic in doctrine and practice. During my first visit, I was immediately impressed by their vision; however, upon closer examination, I noticed that all their vision statements included the term "apostolic." A sampling of the community revealed that this vital target group had no idea what the term meant, and even a great number of the organization's members were unsure of the intended meaning. This organization had a God-given vision reflected in its sound community development objectives. It incorporated the needs of family and singles; however, their vision statement and goals were not user friendly. The drawback was that the terminology, even though correct, stood in the way of clarity. The terminology was that of a seminary graduate and not the language of the intended target group.

The local governmental agencies of the area had grants available to faith-based organizations that were willing to work with at-risk families and were searching for suitable groups, hoping to forge partnerships. The apostolic ministry had a similar program in its vision; however, its terminology prevented clear recognition. Even though the leadership team understood the vision, possible partners and donors could not make the connection. God gives us a clear mandate; however, for the transmitting of that mandate to others, we must communicate properly. This responsibility is a top priority. When this happens, even small organizations are in position to receive greater support, including funding for projects. It is very important to understand that a great portion of your funding may very well come from the corporate groups and government agencies by way of grants and community-based initiatives.

After a weekend workshop, a newly worded vision statement emerged. This vision statement was produced in a variety of forms; each form spoke clearly to its targeted group. Today, even the boys and girls in the children's ministry know and understand the vision of the organization.

The apostolic group secured a local government and a state grant. For a number of years now, the organization has successfully operated a summer program for at-risk families.

Here is another example. Many years ago, while serving as the chairman for a community-based youth center and delivering a regular fundraising presentation, I was introduced to an interesting corporate marketing principle. In the middle of the presentation, the president of a multi-million-dollar company interrupted me. He asked two simple questions:

1. How many children do you reach each year?

2. How many hours of service do you provide to those children?

The amount of the donation hinged on the answer to those two questions. At the conclusion of the meeting, he explained the concept. The success of his company is directly linked to how many customers they have and how many hours the customers use their products. Their goal each year is to:

- Maintain or improve the quality of the product.
- Maintain current customers and gain new ones.
- Increase the advantages to the customers for more frequent use of the products.

Customers + Hours = More Products = More Revenue. He offered funding to our youth center and stated that continual funding would be based on increased number of kids and contact hours each year, while maintaining or improving our product (programs). Companies, donors, and successful people want a measurable vision. *How many people do you envision affecting? How much time will you invest in them? And how will it all grow throughout the years?*

Make it clear, keep it visible, and communicate properly to your target groups, and you will have an effective bridge from your vision to the heart of others. This will secure influence and increase opportunities for continued success.

The personal study section has been provided in an effort to provide questions and activities for critical thinking. Please complete and log your work in a journal. You may also wish to use the material in a small-group setting as a training module for your leaders. This will give you a working format for gathering the information needed for building your vision. If you attend our "Building Your Vision" workshop, bring your completed journal for quick references and discussion.

Personal Study

A Clear Vision

Session Topic: In this session, you will review some components of a clear vision and complete a research assignment.

Practical Wisdom Discovery

1. What is the author's definition of "vision"? How does it differ from yours?
2. What are the major differences between the saved and lost societies?
3. What is one aspect of the Kingdom vision? Give an example of how this can be accomplished through your ministry.
4. What four things will a clear vision do? Can you name a fifth?
5. Do you see terminology concerns in your vision statements? If yes, what are they?
6. How important is influence and why? Give an example of a person of influence in your community and explain how he/she is influential.

Assignment: Research organizations and ministries on the Internet or by other means. Look for and list five that have a clear vision statement. State what their statements have in common.

Prayer Focus:

- Pray that God will give you wisdom in developing and presenting a clear vision.
- Take time to praise and thank God for calling you to ministry.
- Pray for the advancement of the Kingdom of Heaven throughout the earth.

Pray These Scriptures This Week

Psalms 32:8 Proverbs 4:18 John 10:3, 4 Romans 12:2

A Challenging Vision

Vision: Clear, Challenging, and Future Focused

> "A blind man's world is bounded by the limits of his touch; an ignorant man's world by the limits of his knowledge; a great man's world by the limits of his vision."[3] E. Paul Hovey

A vision must be challenging. A challenge is a call to engage in a contest, fight, or competition. A good vision actively challenges people. It calls them to engage in noteworthy endeavors. It does more than build excitement for the moment; it stretches the thinking and faith of individuals and groups. A challenging vision addresses the needs and hopes of both the saved and lost societies. A challenging vision conveys a part of God's passion for His creation.

Attraction

Often, those in a community will be attracted to a part of an organization's vision, and it will become a drawing force resulting in support and commitment for the vision through sustained involvement.

Members of the saved society may join in and support a ministry, program, or outreach of the organization. For para-church ministries, this is important because they depend heavily on volunteers and ministry partners. Unlike local churches, para-church ministries as a rule do not receive tithes and normally do not have a membership.

Members of local churches may see in the vision something that speaks to their area of calling, and this may result in a ministry partnership with them and their local church. Remember, you have more than an organizational para-church or local church vision; you have a Kingdom vision. It has no borders or limitations. One of the intentions of *Kingdom Partnerships* is that it will be beneficial both ways.

As an organization, The CTC Network enjoys the advantages of ministry partnerships in the Caribbean, North America, and Africa. We are not in competition but rather called to complement. We understand and embrace the value of partnerships. From a partnership, both groups are to emerge stronger. It produces a win/win situation and forges a team united in purpose. Here are two well-known acronyms for team. *T*ogether *E*ach *A*chieves *M*ore or *T*ogether *E*veryone *A*chieves *M*ore. A challenging vision is designed to accomplish these and more.

IDENTIFICATION IS A DRAWING CARD

When someone identifies with the overall vision, or even part of it, you will have increased your opportunities to partner, and through this partnership reach the lost society with the gospel of the Kingdom. Often, this attraction and identification will lead to inquiries and possible commitments to the Lord Jesus Christ as Savior. The challenging vision then must speak to concerns outside the organization's walls. I have found that people will support a challenging vision if they believe the following:

1. It will benefit them, their loved ones, and the less fortunate.
2. It provides a hope of succeeding through well-defined action steps.
3. It will make the community a safer place.
4. It will make the world a better place.

5. It welcomes network partners.
6. It is God ordained.

The vision, in order to be challenging, must be bigger in scope than any one person or organization; it must invite others to join in its objectives. It must challenge one to a place of commitment, and it must embrace present and projected needs, offering believable solutions.

Often, a challenging vision speaks to all stages of human development. It takes into account people's needs and concerns at different levels. It allows no one to fall through the cracks. Remember, an organization does not have to plan to achieve it all alone. Look to others and their areas of expertise. This is the networking or partnering aspect of your vision.

A challenging vision provides possible stakeholders with the opportunity to grip a set of principles and core values that will reshape and redefine their lives. To get people to follow, a leader must be able to attract and inspire others. Seeing the possibility of the organization's vision incorporated into personal, family, and professional life will attract people and assist in securing their commitment. It will say, "This is the preferred way. Walk in it, and see dreams come true and godly purpose achieved."

A challenging vision, among other things, will address faulty thinking patterns as they pertain to faith, family, and finances, and offer biblical truth as the only viable alternative. Too often, we limit others and ourselves by designing neat, small visions.

Here are some *Practical Wisdom* points for developing a challenging vision.

How to Develop a Challenging Vision

Look Within. We must look with in us and ask, *What is God saying? What is God's purpose for my life? What is God's purpose for this organization?* At the outset, let me state that the phrase, "Look

Within," is not meant to imply that we have the answer but that the Godhead, through the work of the Holy Spirit, reveals vision to us primarily from within and that leaders are birthing wombs for God in the earth. Also, "Look Within" implies that recognition and understanding of our unique temperament traits is an indicator of God's plan for our lives.

The Birthing Principle

Jesus said: "He that believeth on me, as the scripture hath said, "out of his belly being shall flow rivers of living water" (John 7:38).

The word "belly" is the Greek word *koilia,* which is also translated "womb."[4] This speaks of birthing, the God-given ability to reproduce.

The Holy Spirit is given to the Christian and Christ's Church in order to birth God's purpose or vision in the earth. When the disciples asked the Lord to teach them how to pray, He gave them and us by extension what is commonly called the Lord's Prayer. A part of that prayer states, "Thy kingdom come. Thy will be done in earth, as it is in heaven" (Matthew 6:10). God desires to birth in the earth what is conceived in heaven.

As a *Practical Wisdom* guideline, I pay great attention to godly vision-related thoughts that continually resurface in my thinking process. I write them down and commit them to our Heavenly Father in prayer. I have found that over time these thoughts are presented with opportunities for birthing. It is important to remember that the Holy Spirit does not fill a blank mind. He influences our thoughts. He leads and guides. When a mind is blank and it becomes controlled by another, that is called *possession*, and that is not the workings of God.

In Revelation 22:1, 2, it reads:

> And he showed me a pure river of water of life, clear as crystal, proceeding out of the throne of God and the Lamb. In the mist

> of the street of it, and on either side of the river, was there the tree of life, which bare twelve manner of fruits, and yielded her fruit every month: and the leaves of the tree were for the healing of the nations.

Jesus is that source of life; He reaches the nations by His healing touch. He accomplishes this through the ministry of the Holy Spirit and with vessels of clay, which we are. It is His vision, conceived in heaven, birthed through the womb of the church and its leaders, and fully realized by the work of the Holy Spirit.

We are often guilty of looking up when some answers and pointers of direction are already within us. If we look in the right places, we will discover the God-given vision for the ministry entrusted to us.

We must have God-Ideas in order to be successful. The ideas and methods, if they are ours, will surely fail or greatly miss the mark. This will result in an aborting of the vision or the creation of a vision and/or organization that is not of God. Another of those right places to look within is the place called "temperament."

Temperament and Its Importance

"Temperament" is the inborn part of us that determines how we *react* and *interact* with others and the world around us. The perception that we have of ourselves and others is identified by this inborn part. Temperament may be defined as "God's imprint upon each life." Temperament, coupled with coping skills (learned behaviors), is the determining factor in how well we handle life's challenges.

It is imperative that each leader understands the importance of temperament. It is essential to note that, as we look within and identify our God-given temperament and understand its workings, we are closer to identifying the direction of God's purpose for our lives. An example of this would be a person who has a temperament that is outgoing and people oriented would not be a good employment fit in the computer room of an organization. Possible frequent coffee breaks for fellowship and constant telephone calls by this outgoing-temperament employee will surely hinder production and eventually produce low morale in that division.

This employee may be able to modify his behavior and successfully perform on the job; however, the stressors associated with continually functioning outside his comfort zone will probably produce emotional distress, leading to malfunctioning in other areas and settings. However, this employee with adequate training may be the perfect fit for a position in the marketing division, which, by nature, welcomes and thrives on outgoing temperament styles.

Temperament and the Human Spirit

> "The spirit of man is the candle of the Lord, searching all the inward parts of the belly." Proverbs 20:27

The theory of temperament is a means by which a person may understand the inner workings of man (temperament) as designed by God. We all are aware that God is a Spirit. Man is also a spiritual being created in the image and likeness of God.

Man is not a little God but was created after the pattern of his Creator God. Man was created this way so that he would have the aptitude to have and enjoy fellowship with his Creator God.

When Adam sinned, he fell spiritually, and his spirit became separated from or at odds with God's Spirit. He could no longer receive from God through his spirit. This has left a spiritual hunger in man. This hunger for God has driven man in his ignorance to seek fulfillment (seeking to meet his temperament needs) in pleasure, material things, and sometimes in endeavors and pursuits that may be noble but outside of God's will for him.

In man's quest to be reunited with God, he is, in fact, attempting to meet his temperament needs. Both will never be realized until he accepts

Jesus Christ as Savior and begins maturing in the things of God. This is the power of the new birth. Let's continue pondering this thought.

The Spiritual Link

> "But God hath revealed them unto us by his Spirit; for the Spirit searcheth all things, yea the deep things of God." 1 Corinthians 2:10

The spiritual link with God is through the spirit of man. Man's spirit created by God is the well of man's life. His physical, intellectual, and moral life ought to spring from this well. The God-created well lost its ability to flow properly due to the fall of the first Adam; however, it may once again become fully operational through the work of the second Adam, Jesus Christ, our Savior.

When Adam sinned, his soul and spirit were separated from God. Thus he operated apart from the influences of God. This is also true of non-believers today. For the non-believer, it is his will as opposed to God's will that determines his decisions and actions.

> For from within, out of the heart of men, proceed evil thoughts, adulteries, fornications, murders, thefts, covetousness, wickedness, deceit, lasciviousness, an evil eye, blasphemy, pride, foolishness: all these evil things come from within and defile the man. Mark 7:21-23

Unbelievers, in an attempt to meet their temperament needs, can only draw from areas of the soul and are regulated to the use of humanistic methods. The unbeliever and carnal believer attempt to meet their temperament needs through ways that are in violation to God's Word and wishes. The unregenerate or carnal person can only draw from a compromised well.

Cast away from you all transgressions, whereby ye have transgressed; and make you a new heart and a new spirit: for why will ye die?
Ezekiel 18:31

Believers are able to draw from the spirit and use God-influenced methods. Salvation, or the New Birth, allows man to receive once again from God and results in the knowledge and ability to meet temperament needs in a God-honoring manner. The redeemed receive a new (restored) heart, or temperament, that is now being influenced by God. It is new or restored in the sense that it is now capable of functioning as initially intended. The linking device between the soul and spirit of man is often called the heart of man. It has been stated by some that the heart of man is his temperament, and I believe this to be so.

Let Us Now Put This All Together As It Relates to Temperament and Vision

The Gospel of Matthew records these words of Jesus:

> Come unto me, all ye that labour and are heavy laden, and I will give you rest. Take my yoke upon you, and learn of me; for I am meek and lowly in heart: and ye shall find rest unto your souls. For my yoke is easy, and my burden is light. Matthew 11:28-30

These verses of Scripture are important to understanding the role that temperament plays in determining God's vision for the leader's life and ministry. Here is a brief look at each verse in a *Practical Wisdom* manner.

> "Come unto me, all ye that labour and are heavy laden and I will give you rest" (verse 28).

Leaders become exhausted and weighed down when they try to serve and please the Lord and others in their own wisdom and operate in areas outside of their strengths. When we attempt to be what we are not and do what we should not, exhaustion takes its toll spiritually, mentally, physically, and emotionally. We become guilty of carrying burdens and being saddled with loads that were not intended for us to bear. This heavy burden often leads to failure and burnout and is becoming commonplace in organizations. How can a leader avoid this tragic end?

"Take my yoke upon you and learn of me…" (verse 29).

Yokes were wooden frames placed on the backs of draft animals to make them pull in tandem. When one animal was outfitted for a yoke, it would be designed so that the animal could pull the load easily. The simple yoke consisted of a bar with two loops of either rope or wood that went around the animal's neck. When two animals were pulling a load, the yoke was designed for each to carry its share equally.

As a carpenter, Jesus Christ would have been familiar with the fitting of these yokes for animals. In His time and culture, carpenters built more yokes than houses.

The word "yoke" is used most often in the Bible to speak of slavery and hardships. However, here Christ uses it in a positive way. The yoke is God's will for your life. He has a will for each and every person. It is vital for the leader to understand this truth. God has a definite plan and purpose for your life. He also has a vision for your organization. Success in ministry often occurs when we minister side by side with others, each outfitted with their own yoke. "And he gave some, apostles; and some, prophets; and some, evangelists; and some, pastors and teachers" (Ephesians 4:11). We are designed to carry our load (purpose) and together fulfill God's vision.

"For my yoke is easy, and my burden is light" (verse 30).

The word "easy" may be translated as "well fitting." God has a purpose for the leader's life that is a perfect fit. The yoke, or will, is well fitting because our temperament is designed for the purpose. Here we may ponder which comes first, the purpose or the temperament, the vision or the leader. I believe God first determines the purpose, which is His yoke for our lives, and then places within us at or before birth our unique temperament traits. They are fashioned just for the individual and take into account the leader's projected physical capabilities, spiritual maturity, and emotional makeup.

Have you ever observed the life of another in ministry and wondered how he was able to accomplish or endure what he did? A well-fitted yoke and temperament is part of the answer. Each person's unique temperament is an indicator of where his call may be and what God's mission for his life will entail. It all fits perfectly.

Paul shares this nugget of truth with his protégé, Timothy, as regarding God's call: "Who hath saved us, and called us with an holy calling, not according to our works, but according to his own purpose and grace, which was given us in Christ Jesus before the world began" (2 Timothy 1:9).

God's direction for our lives can be brought into focus through an understanding of our temperament and its traits. Our purpose and direction were determined before the world began. We are encouraged to come and learn from Jesus. We were all fashioned with a special genetic material. God gave King David keen insight into this concept. Read this Scripture prayerfully.

> For thou hast possessed my reins: thou hast covered me in my mother's womb. I praise thee; for I am fearfully and wonderfully made: marvelous are thy works; and that my soul knoweth right well. My substance was not hid from thee, when I was made in secret, and curiously wrought in the lowest parts of the earth. Thine eyes did see my substance, yet being unperfect; and in thy book all my members were fashioned, when as yet there was none of them. Psalm 139:13-16

Each one of us was fearfully and wonderfully made. God knows the end from the beginning. With His unlimited knowledge and wisdom, He fashioned us each in a unique way and for a specific purpose.

Your temperament is the foundation of your makeup. Here is a practical example. God spoke to Noah and stated that He was going to destroy the world with a flood. He also said that He would save Noah, his family, and quantities of animals. How was He going to do this? Well, God instructed Noah to build an ark. God gave him the plan for the ark that would accomplish the mission (Genesis 6:1-22).

The design would be the temperament. The temperament is the design that would make the mission possible. The ark was fitted with a temperament that would ensure its ability to withstand the various challenges. Remember, we were designed and fashioned to fulfill vision or purpose, not the other way around.

As we learn of the Lord Jesus Christ, we begin to embrace that which God embraced us for. Seek the Father in prayer and relationship to discover that vision which complements your temperament so well. As leaders let us be vigilant to:

- Understand, appreciate, and flow in our unique temperament traits.
- Submit to the Lord Jesus Christ and His purpose for our lives and organizations.
- Surrender all ungodly ways of meeting our temperament needs and replace them with methods that are in harmony with the teachings of Scripture.

It is important to understand that we are stewards, or managers, of the gifts with which we are entrusted. We own nothing. Therefore as managers, we are to oversee what God places in our care. This is also true of vision. If it is God-given, we are responsible to God and God alone for its development and full realization. Look within and see the potential that the Lord has placed there, and allow the Holy Spirit to teach and guide you in the development of that potential.

In almost all of my training workshops I incorporate the use of profiles. These profiles help identify temperament and spiritual gifts. I have found the identification of these and teaching on them to be necessary for effective leadership development.

> A special note here for parents and counselors. Assisting children in understanding their temperament traits will provide them with suitable career choices. Often, as parents, we attempt to live vicariously through our children. They must fulfill God's will, not ours.

How to Develop a Challenging Vision (Continued)

Look Around. What is God doing in the earth today through the obedience of others? It is always good to mark obedient servants of the Lord. Observe how they succeed in the mist of their challenges. Hang around them with the aim of learning from their experiences. Do not be afraid to ask questions of people with vision who are successful. I am always interested in associating with people who are already at the level where I desire to be. I have also found that successful people will not seek you out; you must go looking for them and attach yourself to them. *Here is a biblical example:*

> And Elijah took his mantle, and wrapped it together, and smote the waters, and they were divided hither and thither, so that they two went over on dry ground. And it came to pass, when they were gone over, that Elijah said unto Elisha, Ask what I shall do for thee, before I be taken away from thee. And Elisha said, I pray thee, let a double portion of thy spirit be upon me. And he said, Thou hast asked a hard thing: nevertheless, if thou

> see me when I am taken from thee, it shall be so unto thee, but if not, it shall not be so. And it came to pass, as they still went on, and talked, that, behold, there appeared a chariot of fire, and horses of fire, and parted them both asunder; and Elijah went up by a whirlwind into heaven. And Elisha saw it, and he cried, My father, my father, the chariot of Israel, and the horsemen thereof. And he saw him no more: and he took hold of his own clothes, and rent them in two pieces. He took up also the mantle of Elijah that fell from him, and went back, and stood by the bank of Jordan; And he took the mantle of Elijah that fell from him, and smote the waters, and said, Where is the Lord God of Elijah? And when he also has smitten the waters, they parted hither and thither: and Elisha went over. 2 Kings 2:8-14

Elisha recognized what God was doing through Elijah. He made an effort to position himself for the opportunity of promotion to another level of leadership and ministry in an effort to contribute in a more significant way to the building of God's Kingdom. He recognized the season on God's calendar and desired to fully embrace it. You need to ask yourself, *What season is it on God's calendar, and do I have the faith and courage to walk in this present move of God?*

It is wise for leaders to seek out those who are experiencing a move of God in their organizations or ministries. One of the more common mistakes that inexperienced leaders make is that they are anticipating that experienced leaders will seek them out and offer to mentor them. This just does not regularly happen. One who desires to be mentored should initiate the contact; be an Elisha, attach yourself and know that some things are caught, not taught.

What resources are available to me?

As you look around, ask yourself what resources are available to you for realizing the vision. I always consider these two: people and funding. Here are my thoughts on the two.

Three Important Groups

There are at least three people groups that you should be interested in at this time in the development of your vision.

Target Group

The target group is the group that you are attempting to reach through the efforts of your organization or ministry. They are the primary reason for the vision. Your target group's needs and concerns will greatly influence the timing and mission aspects of the vision. As you observe this group, you may wish to look for the answers to the following questions:

- What is God saying about this group?
- What needs and concerns are obvious?
- What appear to be the future needs and concerns?
- What are their cultural and economic diversities?
- What are the developmental trends of this community?

It is important to look at your settlement, town, city, nation, mission field, or workplace ministry through the eyes of the Lord with a view toward community transformation. You must fully commit to what God reveals as your mission.

The Jonah Syndrome

The story of Jonah reveals the heart of Jonah. Jonah was surprised and upset at how God viewed Nineveh. Jonah concluded that he wanted nothing to do with the assignment. He attempted to flee the presence of God and turned his back on the call (Jonah 1:1-3). You must see your target group as God's group and see God's mandate as a command. It is interesting to note that God not Jonah choose the target group. If left to us, we would be very selective and noncommittal. God can give you the required courage to fulfill the mission and unconditional love for His target group. God has a plan for them. His plan includes redemption and restoration. Obedience and compassion are mandatory for the visionary leader.

Workers

Every work needs workers. We are all aware that the vision cannot be accomplished by the visionary leader alone. As your clear and challenging vision attracts potential workers, it will be wise to discern into which category each falls. This process may take time; however, I have discovered that at least two categories of workers are connected to the vision:

1. *Permanent Folk.* Permanent Folk are undeviating people. They are there with you to the end. It is these that you trust over time with leadership responsibilities coupled with authority. Experience has proven that all who start out with an organization will not end with it. *Permanent Folk* stay throughout all the seasons of ministry. They even *hang* in there during the financially and spiritually bitter winters. They are stable stakeholders in the vision. Allocate a great deal of your time and energies for this group. Your sons and daughters in the gospel will emerge from their ranks. Some may physically move on and minister in other parts of the vineyard, but all will stay spiritually connected. The renowned Bahamian Baptist clergyman, Dr. Charles Saunders, once told me he calls this group "The Remnant"; this term about sums it up.

2. *Temporary Folk.* One of the new "buzz" terms used to describe temporary ministry workers or members is the term "scaffolding." Scaffolding people serve a purpose, but it is in regard to building or launching the organization, ministry, or an aspect of the vision. They are like scaffolds placed around a physical construction site. When the project is completed and the building is erected, they are gone. There are at least three types of scaffolds. The first are God-Sent; they have a calling and gift from the Lord to assist organizations. They are Kingdom builders and are used to launch, repair, and prepare organizations for future successes. They are often multi-talented and have the ability to train. The second set is individuals who have careers that are transitory in nature. My friend, Pastor Ernie DeLoach, has mastered the fine art of managing transient workers. The church he pastors is in Key West, Florida, an area that is often called the end of the road. Key West is the last USA community in South Florida and is ninety miles from The Island Nation of Cuba. Key West, with its military base, supplies his church with a steady flow of temporary folk. Many of them provide much-needed worker support for his church and homeless ministry. Expectations for these workers have to be different than those for permanent members of the congregation. The time spent is limited, and their roles are often complementary. However, this arrangement can produce a win-win situation. Temporary workers find a spiritual covering and place to call home with all its advantages. The church is furnished with workers who bring fresh excitement and energy. The third set is those who went and were not sent. They arrive with spiritual and emotional baggage. Bitter toward the leadership of their pervious ministry, they latch on and demand an unreasonable amount of attention. When they leave you, they often state that you and the organization changed and they no longer feel comfortable; however, some of these precious people do find balance

and become contributing members of the Kingdom of God. I have made the grave mistake of appointing scaffolding people to permanent leadership roles only to become overburdened by their drawbacks and eventual departure. What should be your attitude toward *Temporary Folk*? I thank the Lord for these three Temporary Folk types/groups and minister to them, assisting in their development where it is appropriate while keeping an eye toward developing leaders from the *Permanent Folk* for the future stability of the organization. Pray and ask for discernment as to the categories and roles of your workers and what your response ought to be.

Gleaners

To glean means to collect, pick up, gather, assemble, bring together, and scrape together. Gleaners understand that in order to be successful in their field, they need to associate with successful people in other fields. In these associations you glean ideas and principles. Frequently, more is caught (gleaned) than taught. It is important not to only have gleaners but to also *be* a gleaner.

In 1999, forty persons from around the globe were selected by the United States of America to participate in a special fact-finding mission that would take them to twenty USA cities in thirty days. I was selected to represent The Commonwealth of The Bahamas. In this group were medical doctors, nurses, politicians, educators, psychologists, law enforcement personnel, and the princess of the State of Kuwait. I was the only preacher in the entire group. Those three weeks were an educationally enriching period in my life. Being in the sustained company of those successful individuals presented numerous gleaning opportunities. I listened more than I spoke and was observing more than listening. If you wish to be successful in your chosen field, and we all do, it is beneficial to mingle with those who are successful in other fields. Many of the planning and developmental strategies employed by other professionals have great value for ministry leaders and the organizations they lead. Today, that cross-pollination experience is still paying dividends. It is vital to look around; nothing happens in a vacuum and without others. Some of them were apparently gleaning also; at the end of the trip, three persons were voted to speak on behalf of the group at the debriefing and wrap-up session in Washington. I was one of the three. What an honor and privilege that was. Let me reiterate my simple gleaning formula: *Listen more than speaking, and observe more than listening.*

Funding

"And the lord commended the unjust steward, because he had done wisely: for the children of this world are in this generation wiser than the children of light" (Luke 16:8).

Funding is a growing concern for many organizations and ministries. The Bible contains much instruction on money issues. As a matter of fact, it contains more than 2,350 verses dealing with money and/or possessions. Financial concerns are addressed in the Scriptures as they pertain to both spiritual and practical matters. I advise that you conduct an in-depth Bible study on God's perspective on money. This study will prove enriching for you and your leadership team.

Have you considered how you will fund the vision? Funding may have to come from a number of sources. Many organizations spurt, run out of gas, and drift to a halt right here. Truly, if God gives the vision, He will give the *pro*vision. This is true, but how is the funding generated? If you are a local church, basic funding will probably be realized from tithes and offering. Para-church ministries traditionally look to faith pledges, estate giving, and fundraisers. Are there any other avenues?

I wish to offer some, and be warned, they might sound way out there. They might require a temporary shift in your thinking process.

Financing and Its Purpose

One of the more popular phrases in respect to giving that we hear is "sow a seed." It has achieved its popularity mainly through the international media ministries. If you need healing, sow a financial seed; if you do not have all the funds to pay a bill, sow what you have and God will provide what you need. I am aware of the reasoning behind this thinking; however, there was a man spoken of in the Bible that sowed money; well, maybe not sowed, but he did put it right in the ground and was rebuked by his master.

> For the kingdom of heaven is as a man traveling into a far country, who called his own servants, and delivered unto them his goods. And unto one he gave five talents, to another two, and to another one; to every man according to his several ability; and straightway took his journey. Then he that had received the five talents went and traded with the same, and made them other five talents. And likewise he that had received two, he also gained another two. But he that had received one went and digged in the earth, and hid his lord's money. Matthew 25:14-18

The above Scripture reveals that two traded on the money and gained a one hundred percent return, one hid the money in the earth. I think a Kingdom rule here is double what you receive. Faithfulness, discipline, timing, creativity, calculated risk taking, and an understanding of the trading and investment markets are required for a one hundred percent return. Let me present a time-tested financial principle that accomplishes this. It is called *The Rule of* 72, or *The Rule of the Wealthy.*

Investment brokers teach their clients *The Rule of* 72, which is actually a simple formula used for calculating how many years it would take for funds invested to double. Here's how it works:

1. Figure out the annual interest rate on your investment

2. Divide the interest rate into 72
3. The result is the number of years it will take for your investment to double

Here's an Example. Your organization invests fifty thousand dollars in a mutual fund or stock that pays an annual return of ten percent.

1. $50,000
2. 10% annual return
3. 72 divided by 10 = 7.2 years
4. Outcome: $50,000 would double and become $100,000 in 7.2 years

The Bahamas is a tiny nation with a population slightly over three hundred thousand and finds it difficult to secure funding for national youth and sporting programs. We have an ongoing national debate on the positive and negative implications of establishing a national lottery. I object to the concept of a national lottery but offered the following alternative.

Bahamas Youth Foundation

The Bahamas Youth Foundation can be established by receiving a portion of the fees that international and local businesses pay to operate in The Commonwealth of The Bahamas. These funds will be placed in the foundation and diversely invested. Over time, a national budget can be established for youth and sporting organizations. It meets a pressing need and provides for accountability, while easing the burden carried by a few corporate sponsors. I believe this is a Kingdom principle. Many Christian organizations and ministries face a similar predicament. As Christian organizations and ministries, our fundraising techniques must alien themselves to Scriptural standards.

> Then he which had received the one talent came and said, lord, I knew thee that thou art an hard man, reaping where thou hast not sown, and gathering where thou hast not strawed: And I was afraid, and went and hid thy talent in the earth: lo, there thou hast that is thine. His lord answered and said unto him, Thou wicked and slothful servant, thou knewest that I reap where I sowed not, and gather where I have not strawed: Thou oughtest therefore to have put my money to the exchangers, and then at my coming I should have received mine own with usury.
> Matthew 25:24-27

His lord basically said, "Wicked and lazy man, at least put it in the bank and let it gain compounded interest; at least do the minimum requirement of good stewardship." It is important to note that regular savings or fix deposits are only one type of investing; as a matter of fact, the servant's lord implied that it was the least valued form. Seeing that he did not even do this, what he had was taken away and given to the one who had obtained the greater amount. God does reward productivity. As leaders, it is imperative that we understand the mindset of our master (God) and handle His money His way. The average leader is not an expert on financial matters but ought to be one on knowing where to find an expert.

I believe that God has in the workplace believers who are capable and willing to teach the Body of Christ how to invest properly. They are gifted individuals with expertise in business and investing and have a genuine love for the Lord, His church, and the lost society. These individuals for the most part are overlooked by leadership, and their gifts are underutilized. We need to better tap into these resources.

We need to trade more than sow. Wouldn't it be great to be in a position to give or invest in the Kingdom of Heaven not looking for a blessing? Let me put it another way. How would you like to be in a position to give, and it would not change your lifestyle? And I mean give substantively. How would you like for the organization entrusted to you to have a residual income? Or have a financial pipeline (a residual income or pipeline that produces a continual flow of funds derived for businesses and investments as opposed to the solicitation methods that have become common practice for many organizations and ministries)?

Working this Concept

Some years ago, I was appointed operations director for a Florida-based Christian organization that was deep-seated in debt. It provided an opportunity to experiment with some business ideas. Among other ventures, we:

- Painted homes.
- Pressure cleaned vehicles at statewide auto auctions.
- Rang bells during the Christmas season for the Salvation Army at an hourly rate.

This proved to be an exciting time for the organization. We were stretched and literally took a new shape. All of our ideas and plans were bathed in prayer. During the process, we acknowledged that the Lord was ordering our steps, and over time the debt was eliminated. Today, that organization has reached into the entire state of Florida and also has a presence in its neighboring state of Georgia.

The Prosperity Message

It would appear that the Holy Spirit emphasized the prosperity message the lasted two decades so that the *Body of Christ* would have the financial freedom to take the message of the Gospel of the Kingdom of God throughout the earth. A great percentage of believers are apparently arriving to a different conclusion. Prosperity is seen mostly as a God-sent answer to the prayer and desire for personal wealth and financial freedom. Not much has changed in this decade. This tragic miscalculation is being observed in many nations. In my home country, The Bahamas, it is common for churches to announce their yearly themes. These themes, I believe, depict heart values. Many of the themes speak of believers' prosperity and the year of breakthrough. We are delivering a partial message and helping create wrong conclusions if we do not teach all the reasons for prosperity and breakthrough. Quite frankly, I would not want a single year of prosperity or breakthrough but would want to know how I may tap into it continually for all the right reasons. *Global Evangelism* is one of those reasons.

The Bahamas enjoys political stability and has one of the three oldest parliamentary systems in the region. It has one of the highest standards of living, with the Bahamian dollar being equal to the United States of America dollar. Religiously, we have more churches per-capita than any other nation. Geographically, we are located near the mainline of the USA. My home is about sixty miles from West Palm Beach, Florida. Our location allows for easy access to and from other global destinations. We even enjoy USA Immigration pre-clearance privileges. This means we can clear USA Immigration before leaving our shores. We have much, and God requires much of us (Luke 12:48).

I believe that The Bahamas is one of the greatest little nations in the world and that its overall stability has significant spiritual implications. There is more we can do as a nation to fulfill The Great Commission given to us as a *command* by Jesus Christ (Mark 16:15-18).

As a nation, we have for many years been on the receiving end of mission efforts. We have in many quarters developed a receiver's mentality from construction to short-term mission teams; we often receive and rarely send. I truly believe that the tables must turn. We must play our role in sending out missionaries and Kingdom workers. Here is one of my dreams.

> A North American short-term missions team comprised of teenagers and adults arrive in The Bahamas. During the day, they team with a Bahamian contingent and labor side by side. Each evening they sit side by side for training. The following year, the North American and Bahamian contingent travel as one team to a mission field laboring and training side by side for the Glory of God.

This dream can be repeated with any number of people groups. In the natural, The Bahamas has a history of being a transshipment route, from the slave trade era to prohibition, and from illegal smuggling to legal shipping. Why not transship spiritually? This is The Great Commission mandate and requires a substantial amount of funding. The truth is that God is a God of prosperity, and He desires to bless us abundantly. Abundance is simply more than enough, but what we do with our substance, blessings, and overflow has to do with our understanding of stewardship. We are God's managers, or stewards, accountable to Him. One day we will give a full accounting of our actions and the motives that fuel them.

Observe the advice given to Timothy by the apostle Paul:

> Charge them that are rich in this world, that they be not high minded, nor trust in uncertain riches, but in the living God, who giveth us richly all things to enjoy. That they do good, that they be rich in good works, ready to distribute, willing to communicate. Laying up in store for themselves a good foundation against the time to come, that they may hold on eternal life. 1 Timothy 6:17-19

Grants

A grant is funding normally offered by governmental or state agencies to non-profit organizations for approved projects or programs. Guidelines are set and agreed upon by both parties. Many grants are renewable if the program is successful and the organization adheres to the mandatory procedures. These procedures include but are not limited to areas of personnel, program objectives, and submission of reports. Grants commonly represent public and private partnerships that are in the best interest of the community and its target groups.

In the late 1990s, I had the privilege of being a member of the United States of America's International Visitors Program. The program was designed for persons working in the area of drug rehabilitation. Participants visited rehabilitation centers, prevention organizations, federal agencies, and drug courts. We visited more than thirty centers in no less than twenty USA cities. I was most amazed with two findings:

1. The amount of funding available from the state level for nonprofit organizations. An organization could obtain a listing of the grant-approved programs, complete with mandatory requirements and submission deadlines. One could then write a proposal that aligned itself with an approved program. Grants were issued to organizations that best matched the desired outcome. Many of these grants were never applied for. The Bible declares at least two reasons why God's people and their endeavors come to naught or are destroyed. (1) Where there is no vision (Proverbs 29:18), (2) Where there is a lack of knowledge (Hosea 4:6). Many organizations have vision but are lacking in the knowledge department. Organizations must be more proactive. They should find out what is out there and position themselves for greater success.
2. The organizations with the greatest success rates were the ones that fell in the category called "Faith Based," and the majority of these were Christian organizations. This was the topic of choice every evening over dinner. What an opportunity! I think every night we all secretly dreamed of establishing a ministry in North America. Interestingly, our type visas prevented us from accept-

> ing a job for at least two years from the commencement date of the program. I think someone anticipated our dreams.

Many nations have grant programs. With skill and persistence, organizations can avail themselves to this much-needed funding. There are even grant-writing seminars that persons may attend. Does your vision include community or city transformation? Are you seeing the Kingdom vision? If yes, then review your funding strategies and test the waters.

Much has been presented here on a challenging vision. As you begin your personal study section, you would be wise to address the reasons why you are faced with difficulties in fulfilling the vision entrusted to your group. This upcoming personal study section is designed to commence the process of group dynamics in vision building.

Personal Study

A Challenging Vision

Session Topic: In this session, you will review the aspects of a challenging vision and complete an assignment on ministry funding.

Practical Wisdom Discovery

List six reasons why a person or group may identify with a challenging vision.

1. Describe the birthing principle.
2. Explain in your own words the meaning of "temperament."
3. What people and funding resources do you have in your ministry? List and discuss them with your team.
4. What is your understanding of the term "workplace apostles"? Can you list one in your area?
5. As a ministry group, discuss possible steps for creating a challenging vision.

Assignment: Brainstorm with a select group and come up with creative ways to assist a financially struggling ministry. Remember, you want to trade more than sow.

Prayer Focus:

- Pray for organizations and ministries in your area that are facing a financial crisis.
- Take time to praise and thank God for incoming practical wisdom for these ministries.
- Listen with your inner voice for future direction.

Pray These Scriptures This Week

Psalms 1:1 Psalms 16:7 Acts 6:10 Philippians 4:6

Future Focused

Vision: Clear, Challenging, and Future Focused

Vision is futuristic in nature; it focuses on the organization's desired future state. The vision by its very nature and intent will predetermine the future of the organization or ministry. Pragmatically, the future is unpredictable; however, by having a vision and working towards its realization, an organization, in essence, is creating predictable outcomes. That is what God's vision is attempting to do in your organization. It is setting the course and, if followed, will result in God's predetermined outcome for that vision and organization.

As a result of vision casting and formulation, we are able to see the end product from our present position and then work towards that predetermined future coupled with its desired outcomes.

Our thoughts shape us and result in whom and what we become (Proverbs 23:7). God's thoughts in the form of the God-given vision shapes the future of the organization; it results in what that organization becomes. These thoughts result in action steps, and it is these actions steps that in part create the vision realization. I once shared with a class that I believe everything is created twice. Something is created in the mind first, then physically, or in the spiritual realm then the temporal. Which creation is real or more valid? The first, for the second is really only the physical manifestation of the first. Thoughts create and cause the actions that produce. Jesus gives us an example of this when He stated that whoever looks on a person to lust after that person has committed adultery with that person already in his/her heart (Matthew 5:28). If that person never goes on and commits the physical act, that person still created the misdeed. This is a negative example, but it's vivid. Godly vision must be realized in both the spiritual and temporal realms.

Have you ever wondered what happens to organizations that have no vision or are unaware of God's vision for them? It is organizational suicide at the least to exist with out a vision. Proverbs 29:18 states, "Where there is no vision, the people perish…" Habakkuk implied that thou it tarries we are to wait for it (Habakkuk 2:2). There are a number of reasons why the vision is future focused. Let me share a couple here.

God Is Preparing the Leader

"The thoughts of the righteous are right…" (Proverbs 12:5). God builds the leader first then the organization or ministry. He builds and refines leaders. Often, this takes time. What He is looking for are obedient servants, men and women whom He can trust with His vision. His objective is holiness lived out in righteousness. This returns mankind to his former state before the fall. The mission of Jesus Christ in coming to the earth is partly to restore the righteousness that was lost by mankind through the fall of Adam and Eve in the Garden of Eden.

Righteousness is to be in right standing. A self-righteousness person is in right standing; the problem is that he is in right standing only with himself. To be righteous is to be in right standing with God. Jesus restored us to the place of right standing with the Father by His death on the cross for our sins. "For he hath made him to be sin for us, who knew no sin; that we might be made the righteousness of God in him" (2 Corinthians 5:21).

Abraham the father of the faithful walked in righteousness.

> What shall we say then that Abraham our father, as pertaining to the flesh hath found? For if Abraham were justified by works, he hath whereof to glory; but not before God. For what saith the scriptures? Abraham believed God, and it was counted unto him as righteousness. Romans 4:1-3

God's purpose, or vision, for us can only be truly perceived in our spirit and fulfilled in the earth as we walk in righteousness. Righteousness is not the outward religious acts of man; it has to do with a condition of life and a thinking process.

We are in right standing with our creator by the sacrifice of Jesus Christ, and we walk in that right standing through obedience to the precepts of God. Often, the vision will tarry for us because we have not accepted the responsibility to walk in this received righteousness.

The word "righteousness" is an interesting word. It is the word *dikaiosune*,[5] which is the character or quality of being right or just; it was formerly spelled *rightwiseness* which clearly expresses the intended meaning. It is used to denote an attribute of God. The righteousness of God is essentially the same as His faithfulness and truthfulness. These are attributes that are consistent with His nature and promises. Righteousness is the *rightwiseness* of God, the God-thoughts seen in our behavior. Therefore righteousness is more than a standing, it is also the walk that holiness produces and the holiness that the walk secures. It is our choice to obey or disobey the Words or thoughts of God for our lives. James gave a formula for righteous living: "Submit yourselves therefore to God. Resist the devil, and he will flee from you. Draw nigh to God, and he will draw nigh to you. Cleanse your hands, ye sinners; and purify your hearts, ye double minded" (James 4:7, 8).

Formula for Righteous Living:

- *S*ubmit to God
- *R*esist the devil
- *D*raw close to God
- *C*leanse your hands
- *P*urify your hearts

This is what I call the *SRDCP* plan for righteous living. God cannot use us and fulfill His plan for us and the groups we lead if we do not do the above.

One of the catchy church phrases in The Bahamas is: "God helps those who help themselves." On the surface, this seems correct. Truly, God rewards activity; however, at the core of this statement is a subtle perversion. The truth is that we cannot help ourselves. We must rely totally on His grace, wisdom, and empowerment.

Here are some other catchy statements that reinforce this self-fulfilling notion: "I am a self-made man," or, "I pulled myself up by my own boot straps." They all sound noteworthy and noble; however, the thought behind the statements is the root of the problem.

As parents, we strive to develop our offspring to the place where they can survive in society as independent adults and wonder why often, as adults, they drift away from the Lord. Nation builders seek independence for their territories and then spend a great amount of their time in office seeking to establish alliances. Some strive for independence, others interdependence; yet for the Christian, it ought to be total dependence upon the Lord. This is the way to move forward spiritually.

Many are guilty of attempting to serve the Lord in their own wisdom or the wisdom of others, mixing the commands of God with personal preferred plans. I have been guilty of this. Have you?

As I matured, I came to recognize and appreciate the fact that the best of my strength is worthless unless it is in response to God's bidding. We might, at times, have to act independently of others in ministry, but never are we to be independent of God.

God is and must always be our source of knowledge; He is our *rightwiseness.* We are to be totally dependant upon Him. I am aware that this sounds like insecure child's talk, but the Lord delights in a relationship that is totally faith-dependent. Righteousness is obedient living. It's a place and a process. We need His Word at all times. It is safe to be faithful in the last received Word until He gives a new one.

Everything we think or plan on doing must pass through God's filter. Let Him strain it all. After we receive knowledge from Him, we must walk daily in that knowledge. What we receive may sound like foolishness to others, and at times even to us, but if it is from the Lord, we are to trust His Word and commands. His faithfulness and truthfulness are impeccable. Walk in that received Word of God. As He renews our strength, He also gives us additional knowledge.

Let us draw an example from the earth's first couple.

Genesis 3 tells the story of Adam and Eve's disobedience in eating of the forbidden fruit. God had instructed them not to eat of the fruit that contained the knowledge of good and evil. It was God's plan to fellowship with them each day, providing them, among other things, with the knowledge that He felt was necessary. Adam and Eve gave into the temptation and listened to the voice of Satan.

At the appointed time in the evening, God visited with Adam and Eve; however, they hid themselves because they were aware of their nakedness, a result of the knowledge gained by disobedience. What lesson can be learned here? Verses 8-11 bring the story to a climax.

> And they heard the voice of the Lord God walking in the garden in the cool of the day: And Adam and his wife hid themselves

> from the presence of the Lord God amongst the trees of the garden. And the Lord God called unto Adam, and said unto him, Where art thou? And he said, I heard thy voice in the garden, and I was afraid, because I was naked; and I hid myself. And he said who told thee that thou wast naked? Hast thou eaten of the tree, where I commanded thee that thou shouldest not eat?

Of course, God knew the answers to those three questions:

- Where are you?
- Who told you that you were naked?
- Did you disobey me?

The questions were posed for the sake of Adam and Eve. This act on their part broke the faith-dependency relationship that they enjoyed with their creator. It broke their right standing. It resulted in them becoming unholy. Disobedience alters our position and protection-covering.

Let's apply the *Practical Wisdom* principles discovered in James:

- *S*ubmit to God – Adam and Eve should have obeyed.
- *R*esist the devil – Answer him with the Word of God.
- *D*raw close to God – Adam and Eve should have approached God.
- *C*leanse your hands – Let obedience be seen in your actions.
- *P*urify your hearts – Do not second guess God; that leads to a double mind, and you will become unstable in all your ways. Obedience is one sign of a pure heart.

A faith-dependency relationship is one that looks to the voice of the Lord for direction and to the hand of the Lord for stability; this kind of relationship thrives on the *rightwiseness* of God. For a Christian leader to move in the dynamics of the supernatural, that leader must learn to walk by the Word of God. His actions must be in response to the God-thoughts he receives.

Vision will often tarry because God is attempting to get His servant to this place of obedience. Holiness and righteousness are some results of walking after the precepts of the Lord.

Do not view your waiting period as something designed so that extraordinary or supernatural things may happen; rather view it as a period filled with lessons of and opportunities for obedience. Obedience in our thought patterns is the main objective.

Jesus Christ, in His test just prior to public ministry, replied to the devil, "...Man shall not live by bread alone, but by every word that proceedeth out of the mouth of God" (Matthew 4:4).

As descendants of Adam and Eve, *rightwiseness* must be our fruit of choice. We shall see in our next example that it might take years to get to this place of obedience and a lifetime to maintain it.

Let's learn from Abraham.

> After these things the word of the Lord came unto Abrah in a vision, saying, Fear not, Abrah: I am thy shield, and thy exceeding great reward. And Abrah said, Lord God, what wilt thou give me, seeing I go childless, and the steward of my house is this Eliezer of Damascus? And Abrah said, Behold, to me thou hast given no seed: and lo, one born in my house is mine heir. And, behold the word of the Lord came unto him saying, This shall not be thine heir; but he that shall come forth out of thine own bowels shall be thine heir. And he brought him forth abroad, and said, Look now toward heaven, and tell the stars, if thou be able to number them: and he said unto him, So shall thy seed be. And he believed in the Lord; and he counted it to him for righteousness. Genesis 15:1-6

Abrah received a promise from the Lord and chose to believe the Lord. His believing in God's promise was seen as righteousness. Abrah was in right standing because he chose to align his thinking with God's. He believed, and now he would be called to demonstrate his obedience by walking in the promise.

God had given him a visible image in the stars on which to hold. The stars were to build faith and provide a rallying point. He could look at them any night that his heart was becoming dim through approaching unbelief. He would have his desire of an heir. God was indeed his shield and reward. When would this happen? God did not say. How would it happen? Through his loins the child would come, but through the womb of whom?

Time passed and nothing happened.

> Now Sarai Abraham's wife bare him no children: and she had an handmaid, an Egyptian, whose name was Hagar. And Sarai said unto Abrah, Behold now, the Lord hath restrained me from bearing: I pray thee, go in unto my maid; it may be that I may obtain children by her. And Abrah hearkened to the voice of Sarai. Genesis 16:1, 2

Sarai was in keeping with the custom of that day when she gave Hagar to Abrah as a substitute wife, and Ishmael was born to this union. Abrah, in a faithless state, looked to the culture of his day for the fulfillment of the promise. We need to constantly remind ourselves that the Word of God supersedes culture. God will fulfill His promise His way.

We need to maintain *rightwiseness* even when the vision tarries and other possible solutions present themselves. Some well meaning, familiar, and influential voices will offer you advice and point you in other seemly valid directions, but remember, whatever you create you will have to live with and ultimately give an account to God.

Let's continue with this account.

> And when Abrah was ninety years old and nine, the Lord appeared to Abrah, and said unto him, I am the Almighty God; walk before me, and be thou perfect. And I will make my covenant between me and thee, and will multiply thee exceedingly. And Abrah fell on his face: and God talked with him saying, As for me, behold, my covenant is with thee, and, thou shalt be a father of many nations. Neither shall thy name any more be called Abrah, but thy name shall be Abraham; for a father of many nations have I made thee. And I will make thee exceeding fruitful, and I will make nations of thee, and kings shall come out of thee. And I will establish my covenant between me and thee and thy seed after thee in their generations for an everlasting covenant, to be a God unto thee, and to thy seed after thee. And I will give unto thee, and to thy seed after thee, the land wherein thou art a stranger, all the land of Canaan, for an everlasting possession; and I will be their God. And God said unto Abraham, Thou shalt keep my covenant therefore, thou, and thy seed after thee in their generations. This is the covenant, which ye shall keep, between me and you and thy seed after thee; Every man child among you shall be circumcised. And ye shall circumcise the flesh of your foreskin; and it shall be a token of the covenant betwixt me and you. And he that is eight days old shall be circumcised among you, every man child in your generations, he that is born in the house, or brought with money of any stranger, which is not of thy seed. He that is born in thy house, and he that is brought with thy money, must needs be circumcised: and my covenant shall be in your flesh for an everlasting covenant. And the uncircumcised man child and whose flesh of his foreskin is not circumcised, that soul shall be cut off from his people; he hath broken my covenant. And God said unto Abraham, as for Sarai thy wife, thou shalt not call her name Sarai, but Sarah shall her name be. And I will bless

> her, and give thee a son also of her: yea, I will bless her, and she shall be a mother of nations, kings of people shall be of her. Then Abraham fell upon his face, and laughed, and said in his heart, Shall a child be born unto him that is a hundred years old? And shall Sarah, that is ninety years old bear? And Abraham said unto God, O that Ishmael might live before thee! And God said, Sarah thy wife shall bear thee a son indeed; and thou shalt call his name Isaac: and I will establish my covenant with him for an everlasting covenant, and with his seed after him. Genesis 17:1-19

This is a portion of Scripture that contains a number of vision-action steps. I encourage you to undertake a careful study of this conversation between God and Abraham. Observe the following:

- God instructs Abrah to walk before Him and be mature.
- God presents a covenant to Abrah.
- God changes the names of Abrah and Sarai.
- God promises Abrah and his seed land.
- God institutes circumcision of the flesh of the foreskin. It was to take place when a male child was eight days old. Eight being the number of new beginnings, as if to say that what Abrah produces (seed) must not be of the flesh, it must be covenant seed with God and in response to God's will.
- God promises a son to Abraham and Sarah.
- Abraham laughs in disbelief.
- Abraham asks for God's consideration of Ishmael as the channel for God's purpose.

Verse 19 is very interesting. God says three things to Abraham, and it appears that God is angry:

1. Sarah will bear you a son.
2. You will name him Isaac.
3. I will establish my covenant with *him* and *his* seed.

For the greater part of the conversation, God promises to establish the covenant with Abraham and his seed. Now his immediate promised seed is given a name and is singled out as the one with whom God will covenant. This is food for thought. Is this in response to Abraham's attempt at negotiating, or is it just a declaring of the sequential order of the promise's fulfillment? I believe it is both.

A challenging vision cannot be manifested in vessels that insist on thinking earthly. We have to arrive to the place where we stop fighting God's way and submit to His plan. We all have our fears, preferences, and challenges; however, total obedience toward God in the face of these is required, no matter the consequences. Jesus Christ understood this principle. He uttered this prayer before His arrest and eventual crucifixion. "...O my Father, if it be possible, let this cup pass from me: nevertheless not as I will, but as thou wilt" (Matthew 26:39). This was the heart attitude of Jesus Christ our Savior and example. He was obedient to the will of His Heavenly Father, and we must be too.

Rightwiseness is an absolute for the Christian Leader. God corrects our thoughts. Our godly thoughts correct are walk. Our faulty and fleshly actions are replaced with Christ-like obedience and Holy Spirit-led steps. The foundation on which this all stands is God's Word.

God is Preparing the Season

I have always been intrigued by Jesus' first public miracle; the occasion and need is thought provoking. The account of the turning of water into wine, His first public miracle, is recorded in the Gospel of John.

> And the third day there was a marriage in Cana of Galilee; and the mother of Jesus was there: And both Jesus was called, and his disciples, to the marriage. And when they wanted wine, the mother of Jesus saith unto him, they have no wine. Jesus saith unto her, Woman, what have I to do with thee? mine hour is not yet come. His mother saith unto the servants, Whatsoever he saith unto you, do it. And there were six water-pots of stone, after the manner of purifying of the Jews, containing two or three firkins apiece. Jesus saith unto them; Fill the water pots with water. And they filled them to the brim. And he saith unto them draw out now, and bear unto the governor of the feast. And they bear it. When the ruler of the feast had tasted the water that was made wine, and knew not whence it was: (but the servants which drew the water knew;) the governor of the feast called the bridegroom, And saith unto him, Every man at the beginning doth set forth good wine: and when men have well drunk, then that which is worse: but thou hast kept the good wine until now. This beginning of miracles did Jesus in Cana of Galilee, and manifested forth his glory: and his disciples believed on him. John 2:1-11

Jesus was fully aware that there was a pressing need at the wedding reception. Perhaps it was only the saving of face for the bridegroom, but a need did exist. Jesus' mother knew that her son could fix the problem; however, Jesus reminded her that His hour to reveal Himself publicly had not yet arrived. In simple terms, this was bad timing. Mary never answered Jesus but spoke to the servants in His hearing. Mary used her influence. As leaders, we must be careful how we allow others to influence us.

Some will tend to influence us for their own desires and personal ob-

jectives. Still our love for others can be an influencing factor in our decision-making process. Sometimes a perceived need and a sense of loyalty will persuade us.

Remember, as leaders, we will have to live with the results of our actions and that there is a greater measure of judgment for the leader. Once some wheels are in motion, there is no stopping them. This event unmistakably displays the power of influence.

Please note that the immediate results of this miracle were all positive:

1. A pressing need was met.
2. The governor of the feast was impressed.
3. The faith of the disciples was increased.
4. The bridegroom was pleased.
5. The servants witnessed a miracle.
6. Mary accomplished her goal.
7. Jesus pleased His mother.

However, there are always long-term effects to any action or decision we make as leaders.

In many parts of the world, even to this day, this miracle is a bone of contention. The debate as to whether the wine was fermented or unfermented remains a hot topic. Some use this event to justify the consuming of wine as believers; others have lengthy discussions and present scientific reasons why it had to be unfermented. In some quarters, this has divided families, local churches, and fellowships.

By no stretch of the imagination am I suggesting that Jesus sinned by granting His mother's request. The only sin connected to Him was when He bore the sins of the world on the cross. However, by His own volition, He suggested that it was bad timing. This was the season for Jesus' public ministry, but was it the right time, place, and fashion in which to launch it?

It is important for leaders and organizations to move in their season and on time. The book of Ecclesiastes 3:1 declares, "To every thing there is a season, and a time to every purpose under the heaven."

The word "season" is from the Hebrew word "Zeman," which means "an appointed time." God has an appointed time for us in nature. There are also appointed times spiritually and for our endeavors. Scientists have tried to improve on the natural cycle of nature. With crops, poultry, and beef, they have sped up the maturing process. Why? Because of demand and greed, we have altered and changed systems. Many leaders attempt this same feat, maybe for other reasons than those listed; however, this action can alter God's vision. I have been guilty of this blunder.

In my first few years of ministry, I sensed that the Lord had called me to an itinerary ministry. God spoke to my heart that I would have a ministry base from where I would travel to and from the nations. He even showed me the land that would be the operational base. I could not wait for His timing. The first opportunity I got, I purchased a different parcel of land and built by faith (yes, by faith) a house that would serve as my base of operations. During the first phase of the construction, a project that took three years because we were building by faith, I had a dream concerning the house. In the dream, the house was at the foundational level and remained there. I was convinced that this was an attack from the devil and did not recognize the rebuking of the Lord. I finished the house, and we never spent one night in it. We had to practically give it away. The amount received was used to put the down payment on the land and house that God showed me would be our base. This painful process took eleven years.

There is an appointed time for a vision. It is the time when natural and supernatural things seem to happen; it is ultimately a time of fruit bearing. This fruit-bearing time is when it all seems to flow without much effort on our part. We meet the right people; doors of opportunity open and often funding problems seem to disappear, excitement is high, and favor is apparent in the appointed time for a vision.

It is during the appointed time that fruit is being manifested in our organizations and vision is being realized. The appointed time is God ordained and must be man perceived. The appointed time for reaping is associated to our time of vision sowing and seed planting.

Seasons and Times

Our first missionary assignment was on one of our family islands in The Bahamas. Those were lean years for the islanders, and I had to, along with others, avail myself to some farming for survival; every watermelon and tomato counted. A seasoned farmer took me under his wing and taught me how to identify seasons and times. On the back of every seed envelope were the dates for the season to plant the crop; however, there is a time in the season which, if the seed is planted, will produce the largest fruit possible, not in numbers, but in individual size. Understanding and committing to this would give me the greatest bang for my dollar.

The Time of the Full Moon

The seasoned farmer pointed out that if the right seeds for the season were planted during the days of a full moon, the fruit would be quite large—larger than normal. There is a possible full moon for every organization or ministry. Sometimes the vision tarries because God is waiting for us to plant the seeds of the vision in the full moon time. He wants to ensure that there is the greatest return on the investment and that it has the opportunity to be as grand as He envisions it. There are times when there is nothing wrong with us as the leader or the organization; it is just a matter of timing.

When it is perceived that other factors have to line up or fall in place, we need to wait for the full moon; you will spiritually sense its approaching. It is advisable to patiently wait and look for that full moon time. God's timing is most important; it guarantees success.

While waiting, you may wish to do the following:

- Prepare the soil; this might entail sharing your vision with the right people or investing your time and talents in a group that is accomplishing what you envision.
- Secure the needed training or develop a mentoring program where future leaders will emerge.
- Utilize the waiting season for sustained prayer and fasting.
- Uncomplainingly wait for the Lord to align network partners and necessary circumstances.
- Develop strategies and build spiritual hedges around you and your family.

Spiritual seed planted during a full moon will produce the largest fruit possible. Confidently know that seeds planted in the spiritual full moon will develop and fully mature.

> Our future is surely determined not only by the seeds of the past but also when those seeds were planted.

I look for the full moon opportunities and know that if seeds of *rightwiseness* and *faith* are planted during the spiritual full moon, I will one day harvest a challenging vision. I then understand that there is a waiting process, and I must utilize that waiting season properly. "Though it tarry, wait for it; because it will surely come, it will not tarry" (Habakkuk 2:3).

By faith I must wait for harvest time. Every organization ordained by God is expected to sow and reap good fruit in its appointed time and season. Here are some *Practical Wisdom* points recapped:

- There is a season to plant – Know the Season

- There is a time in a season to plant – Know the Time
- There is a season to reap – Know the Season
- There is a time in the season to reap – Know the Time

Timing is vital. Even on an automobile, if we wish to maximize the power of the engine, we must ensure that its timing is precise. Untimely spurts waste gas and may also cause severe accidents. A marching band knows the value of timing. Stock market brokers understand the law of timing. Baseball players practice timing. We must too!

Prayerfully complete the personal study section. This section will challenge you to interact fully with the material. You are required to complete the assignment with a partner.

Personal Study

Future Focused

Session Topic: In this session, you will explore the concept of and reasons why a vision is future focused.

Practical Wisdom Discovery

1. List and discuss at least two reasons why a vision tarries.
2. Explain the *SRDCP* plan for righteous living.
3. What mistake did Abraham make? How can we learn for it?
4. Do you think Jesus felt pressured at the marriage in Cana? Give at least two reasons for your answer. Discuss a similar situation that you have encountered.
5. Explain the full moon concept.
6. Why is timing important to you? Fully explain.

Assignment: Discuss with a friend the conversation between God and Abraham. Pay special attention to God's instructions. Compare your thoughts and write down your conclusions.

Prayer Focus:

- Pray asking God for the courage to remain obedient.
- Take time to praise and thank God for His faithfulness.
- Listen with your inner voice for correction from the Lord.

Pray These Scriptures This Week

Psalms 103:1 Psalms 34:7 Colossians 3:2 Philippians 4:8

Your Life as a Vapor

> Go to now, ye that say, To day or to morrow we will go into such a city, and continue there a year, and buy and sell, and get gain: Whereas ye know not what shall be on the morrow. For what is your life? It is even a vapour, that appeareth for a little time, and then vanisheth away. For that ye ought to say, If the Lord will, we shall live, and do this, or that. James 4:13-15

James, the brother of Jesus Christ, wrote the epistle of James to the Jewish believers in Christ in his day. James calls them and, by extension, believers everywhere to a life that shows the world in which they live: godly purpose, humility, unselfishness, and love. These are qualities of the spiritually focused and ought to be visible in all believers. The epistle is loaded with *Practical Wisdom* principles and is worth studying in its entirety.

In the above Scripture, James encourages his readers to view their lives as vapors. With this as a foundational principle, he states that it is foolish to plan and pursue anything outside of God's will, emphasizing that one's thoughts and actions must harmonize with God's purpose and providence. We are advised to remember that all plans are subject to God's granted permission and enablement. God's purpose must guide the choices for our tomorrows and will in the end determine our success.

Is It Possible to Know God's Will?

The wonderful reality is that we can and should know God's will and purpose for our lives. His purpose for our very existence is not held as an eternal secret. God by His *Word* has openly declared and decreed His plan and purpose for humankind. By His *Spirit*, He orders the steps of each person, thus establishing a specific role for every life. I believe He shares His purpose for each inquiring mind on a daily basis. Is this not, to a certain extent, the intent of prayer? We discover and bathe His will for us in *prayer* and through submission allow its earthly birth and full development. Often, submission to God in the wilderness of various *circumstances* creates a path toward God's purposeful will for us. His purpose, will, and vision govern and guide the intent of the human heart; they reflect and mirror the pulse of the divine.

James admonishes us that plans are sure, predictable, and successful only as they are in accordance with God's purpose, or will. He uses an analogy of a person's life with that of a vapor, brief and constantly fading. However, upon closer examination we discover that this brief and fading entity has other qualities.

The Essence of Vapor

Webster defines vapor as:

- Moisture in the air, especially *visible*, floating moisture, as light mist.
- Any light, cloudy *substance* in the air, as smoke or fumes.
- Any substance in the gaseous state, which under ordinary conditions is usually a *liquid or solid.*
- A gas *below* its critical temperature.
- That which is *fleeting and unsubstantial.*[6]

By examining the list of definitions for vapor and then applying them to an individual life, we may assume the following:

A person's life is to be *visible*. Each individual life, no matter how brief and seemly insignificant, is designed to be viewed by others. Each life should be visible and transparent. As transparent, it allows greater light to shine through it.

- A person's life is to have *substance*. There is a quality of life that is available and should be commonly observed in all. Each life is to contain spiritual, moral, and social substance. There must also be substance in our goals and depth reflected in our commitments.

- A person's life is to remain *pliable*. Under normal conditions, a person's life may have a definitive shape; however, life is not experienced under normal conditions, therefore it must remain pliable in God's hands.

- A person's life is to be *ignitable*. We are equipped with the capacity to ignite ourselves and others for the glory of God and the betterment of humankind. Each life is a vapor waiting to spark.

- A person's life is to be *absorbed* into the mainstream. Our life must contribute to the development of the Kingdom of Heaven on the earth by working itself into the fabric of society. Each life should leave a positive imprint on the world.

All five of these principles are fully developed in the next book in this series (Practical Wisdom for Understanding Your Life). Here I present a part of the first principle.

A Person's Life Is to Be Visible

A life that is visible ought to be accessible too. It should be fashioned so that it can be seen and touched by all. It is also transparent, allowing greater light to shine through it.

When mom asked my brother and me that pointed question, "What do you wish to do with your life?" she and dad were left with the task of accepting the mission of guiding us in our perceived calls or rejecting the mission and observing the outcome of misguided lives.

What is evident by the teachings of Scripture is that once a person recognizes and responds to the call and further develops passion and knowledge for their endeavors, life then cannot, and must not, be lived in a vacuum that is unrelated to and detached from a global audience. A person's life must be visible.

At age thirteen, my parents undertook a financial and emotional burden by sacrificing a great deal, making it possible for me to attend a military high school in North America. When Mom kissed me goodbye, she whispered in my ear, "Son, please don't get involved in the ethnic and race issues in America. We are sending you there to receive a proper education." This was in the early 70s, and racial tension was very much alive in the south. As a result of a series of events, I did become naively involved on my campus for equality and justice, not in disrespect or disobedience, but in response to working out in daily practice what God was working into my life.

I believe her desire for me to refrain from involvement was because of her deep love for me. Mom was aware that I had some sort of a call upon my life; however, she was equally concerned with my maturity level and limited perceptions. She was, in her own way, saying, "Do not let your passion rob us of you." Her unspoken question may have been, "Can you not live out your purpose without an audience?" I believe at some point in all of our lives we secretly and silently ask this very question. Our love for others coupled with the fear associated with potential loss may hinder complete obedience to the Lord. There are many other reasons why a person may refuse to become visible; here are four things that prevent visibility.

Fear

Fear is an intense dislike or distaste to or apprehension of a person or place, event or activity that causes emotional distress and often avoidance behavior. Because of fear, many will never climb the stage of life, and others have abandoned their stage. Fear is not only an intense dislike, distaste, or apprehension, it is also a spirit that possesses and controls one's life.

We are reminded in Scripture, "...God has not given us the spirit of fear: but of power, and of love, and of a sound mind" (2 Timothy 1:7). The apostle Paul wrote this to Timothy, his son in the gospel. It was written encouraging him and others to remain steadfast in the midst of challenges. By personal experience, Paul knew of the lethal grip of fear. If fear is not from God, from where does it originate? It originates from and is used as a ploy of Satan and has the ability to be a dream and vision killer.

The spirit of fear or apprehension stifles and, if it is left unchecked, eventually eliminates the forward movement of a person, purpose, undertaking, or vision. Fear paralyzes the heart and immobilizes the walk. Some are afraid of failure, while others are afraid of success. Some are trapped by the memories and deeds of the past, while others are afraid of impending change that is most certain. Still others fear rejection, criticism, responsibilities, and the demands that visibility entails.

Fear is faith misdirected and misapplied; by this I mean fear believes that the negative or thing feared will come to pass, and this conviction helps create its reality. "For the thing which I greatly feared is come upon me, and that which I was afraid of is come unto me" (Job 3:25). This renders fear as influential as faith; over time, it develops into a belief system, taking on a mind of its own, thus classified as a spirit.

We overcome fear and neutralize its influence by unwavering faith in God and His Word. By embracing God and His provisions, we are able to operate in the spirit of power, love, and a sound mind.

Familiarity

Familiarity is thorough knowledge and understanding of something. There are those who will never move forward in a vision or mandate from the Lord because they are too familiar with a person, place, or project. They allow their familiarity with any one of these to hinder them from viewing their position from a purely spiritual vantage point.

Familiarity hindered the Old Testament preacher Jonah. He was displeased that God wished to extend the opportunity for forgiveness toward the wicked city of Nineveh. Jonah's familiarity with the nature of the city and his self-righteousness resulted in him rebelling and attempting to flee God's presence and providence. By a series of events, God brought him to the place of accepting the call to visit and preach at Nineveh. God made him known on the ship in order to make him visible in the city (Jonah 1:1-7).

Like Jonah, our human knowledge is often in conflict with divine grace and preference. Familiarity often leads to prejudging and results in disobedience and consequently missed opportunities for the kind of success derived from pleasing God.

Familiarity may also cause one to be rejected by the community. Jesus could do only a few miracles in His hometown because of unbelief (Matthew 13:58). Familiarity here overshadowed opportunity and produced an unbelief that nullified potential miracles. Familiarity applied as a negative virtue by His community produced this unbelief.

There will be those who will flat out reject you and the message you share simply because you are too familiar. Perhaps they knew you as a youth, or they observe flaws in your character. Many will embrace unknown ministers and leaders for guidance, somehow thinking a word from a stranger is more authentic. This will happen, but never let it be said that *you* missed a God-inspired opportunity because of familiarity. There are those in shouting and viewing distance that the Lord of the Harvest is using mightily; do not allow familiarity to overshadow your opportunity for success. S*ee* Christ in them, and let others *see* Christ in you.

Failure

Failure is anything unsuccessful. We all have failed at one thing or another, whether it is family, marriage, parenting, business, career, hobbies...the list may very well be endless. We have also, to varying degrees, failed God in our personal lives. All are guilty of falling short of the mark of holiness. From the perspective of guilt and shame and engulfed with the pain associated with personal failure, we often wish to be excused from the stage of life. However, even in this wounded state we still sense the call on our lives; dreams may be dim, but they still exist. Hope may be fading, but a flicker of it is still present.

It is certain that every leader must go through a season of trials and testing. The apostle Paul in the Book of Romans went to great lengths explaining the victory over sin that is ours by Christ Jesus. Victory is possible in the midst of any temptation, trial, or test; however, he also acknowledged that believers will have a wilderness experience where they will be tempted and tried with varying success. If and when failure occurs, we are to confess it, repent of it, and seek forgiveness from the Lord and the offended if possible. Psalm 51 gives us a model for recovery from sin. King David's process of repentance contains at least six steps:

1. Acknowledge your sin to yourself. "...I acknowledge my transgressions: and my sin is ever before me" (v. 3).
2. Acknowledge your sin to God. "Against thee, thee only have I sinned and done what is evil in thy sight..." (v. 4).
3. Assert God's faithfulness and forgiveness. "Have mercy upon me, O God, according to thy lovingkindness: according unto the multitude of thy tender mercies blot out my transgressions" (v. 1).
4. Accept your sinful nature as a reality. "Behold, I was shapen in iniquity; and in sin my mother conceived me" (v. 5).

5. Ask God to restore you. "Create in me a clean heart, O God, and renew a right spirit within me" (v. 10).
6. Answer the call to disciple. "Then will I teach transgressors thy ways..." (v. 13).

With godly *confidence, courage, counsel, and compassion* you move forward. God rescues, revives, and restores!

THE PERFECT MODEL

Jesus Christ is our perfect model for overcoming temptations and trials. He proved in His wilderness experience that it is possible to overcome Satan and the desires of the flesh. Jesus Christ, by conformity to and reliance upon the Word of God, came out of His wilderness experience in the power of the Holy Spirit (Luke 4). He endured temptations as a man filled with the Holy Spirit, establishing a spiritual precedent. The work of the cross and the promise of the Father ensure that this same power is available to all believers. I have found great comfort in the fact that Jesus will ask of me nothing that He has not already done, and that He also provides the means for its success.

FATIGUE

Fatigue is exhaustion of strength by reason of toil. It is a weariness that takes over a person. Many leaders are just simply tired. They are drained of energy and consequently fade away from the stage of life. Fatigue may not only be physical; it may be emotional as well as spiritual. Fatigue often occurs when our lives are out of balance, or we have just completed a demanding task. It is at these moments and periods that we are most vulnerable.

A Remedy for a Fatigued Prophet

1 Kings 18 and 19 tells an interesting story of a fatigued prophet. The prophet Elijah had just accomplished two great spiritual victories: the defeat and destruction of the false prophets of Baal and the answered prayer for rain. Afterwards, he received a death threat from King Ahab's wife, Jezebel, and would experience the nadir of fatigue and discouragement. The death threat was powerful in that it painted a visible picture.

> And Ahab told Jezebel all that Elijah had done, and withal how he had slain all the prophets with the sword. Then Jezebel sent a messenger unto Elijah, saying, So let the gods do to me, and more also, if I make not thy life as the life of one of them by tomorrow about this time. 1 Kings 19:1, 2

Alone, exhausted, and concerned for his life, fear gripped his heart and he fled. Weary and depressed, he sat under a tree and requested God to take his life. He wanted off the stage. The mission, isolation, and mounting stress were finally too much to endure. In this state, he inaccurately evaluated the situation and concluded that he was the only one still faithful to God. He no longer was able to see life from God's viewpoint; he was blinded by his challenges and rendered unbalanced by his weariness. What *Practical Wisdom* remedy did God provide for this fatigued leader?

God provided:

- *Rest* – Lengthy and peaceful
- *Refreshments* – Food and drink
- *Regrouping* – Physical activity and spiritual dialogue
- *Reassurance* – God assured him there were still faithful others

- *Resume* – God told him to get back to his mission
- *Relationship* – God made available Elisha for companionship and mentoring

The Value of Balance

> And the apostles gathered themselves together unto Jesus, and told him all things, both what they had done, and what they had taught. And he said unto them, Come ye yourselves apart into a desert place, and rest a while: for there were many coming and going, and they had no leisure so much as to eat. Mark 6:30-31

Jesus understood the value and necessity of and for rest. He instructed His disciples to take a break from ministering and eat and rest. He knew the importance of not allowing the demands associated with ministry to overshadow the basic needs of ministers.

Ministry and leadership are very demanding, and often those to whom you minister will not exercise a conscience. They will press you toward the brink of exhaustion, and this pressing may easily become a runaway train. I recall once being awakened at three o'clock a.m. by a parishioner's telephone call and was asked if I was asleep.

Jesus desired for His disciples to withdraw; however, the people followed them into the desert demanding yet more ministry. His attempt here for balance failed. You must always strive to maintain a balance in your ministry. Design a plan for rest and relaxation, and follow it as much as possible; it will serve you well in the long run. In 2006, I had to make adjustments to my schedule. I was working an average of seventeen hours per workday and started to notice the telltale signs of physical and mental fatigue. Here is a list of my major adjustments:

- Work days were reduced to ten-hour days
- Ministry-related phone calls were routed through the office
- My cell phone was given to our daughter
- Walks on the beach were taken at every possible opportunity
- Phone calls at home were not received after nine o'clock p.m.
- Eating habits were changed
- Time with God, spouse, and family were increased

I basically filled my calendar first with my priorities, and for the first time in twenty-seven years of ministry, I knew what it was like to politely decline a speaking engagement. Here is a thought to consider. When we become perpetually fatigued, our visions are canceled by default.

The Mandate Remains

We are with all of our weaknesses, challenges, and insecurities still required to present ourselves to God and our world as visible servants. We are to be visible in our field of endeavor or chosen career. Our faith must be on display too. It is impossible for a believer to separate his faith from his chosen career, profession, or daily life. When we attempt to live double or separated lives, we run the risk of robbing others of opportunities for wholeness and fulfillment. We are mandated to model Jesus Christ. God never intended for us to live our lives under the radar of an audience; it is selfish and perhaps even cowardly to constantly live to oneself.

We are stewards of the talents and gifts entrusted in our care by our Heavenly Father. We must share and display them; they are not for personal relishing but for the benefit of all. It is not egotistical having a desire to make an impact on your generation. This desire can be accomplished with godly purpose, humility, unselfishness, and love. The grace and gifts of God are sufficient for this quest. We are to become and stay visible for the glory of God and the betterment of the human race. Visibility remains one of the responsibilities of believers.

Jesus stated in Matthew 5:14-16,

> Ye are the light of the world. A city that is set on an hill cannot be hid. Neither do men light a candle, and put it under a bushel, but on a candlestick; and it giveth light unto all that are in the house. Let your light so shine before men, that they may see your good works, and glorify your Father which is in heaven.

We are designed and destined for visibility and must be determined to live out this divine privilege. Many of us are embodied with temperaments or preferences that prefer isolation and solitude; however, we are mandated to be visible.

We are here for a brief moment and are equipped with the ability to fulfill God's purpose on the stage of life. Let that light shine on the dark paths of internal and external human struggles and allow it to point fellow sojourners in the direction of God's divine light, Jesus Christ! This is the *transparent* element of a vapor.

We are transparent when we allow the light of God to shine through; we are visible for His cause and glory. Take center stage and draw attention to the King of kings. Being visible is not a choice; it is a Kingdom of Heaven mandate. Both Matthew and Mark recorded this Kingdom mandate commonly known as *The Great Commission.*

> Go ye therefore, and teach all nations, baptizing them in the name of the Father, and of the Son and of the Holy Ghost: teaching them to observe all things whatsoever I have commanded you:

> and, lo, I am with you alway, even unto the end of the world. Matthew 28:19-20

> ...Go ye into all the world, and preach the gospel to every creature. He that believeth and is baptized shall be saved: but he that believeth not shall be dammed. And these signs shall follow them that believe; In my name shall they cast out devils; and they shall speak with new tongues; they shall take up serpents; and if they drink any deadly thing, it shall not hurt them; they shall lay hands on the sick, and they shall recover. Mark 16:15-18

Believers are commanded to "Go!" We are to be visible. The Great Commission is not just for a select few but for everyone. All believers have received this command and will be held responsible for its fulfillment. As we go about our daily lives in the workplace and leisure place, we are to preach Christ. We are to make Him known.

The Kingdom of God is on center stage in heaven and desires the same on earth. It is to be seen in that grand place on earth through us. Let others choose to remain behind the scenes or join the stage crew for the showing of "Your Life as a Vapor." As for you, take your place among the active participants and execute to the best of your ability; leave your imprint and a godly legacy. Blaze a trail, fulfill divine purpose, and shine as a reflector of Jesus Christ. Know Him in His fullness and make Him fully known through your visible life and organization.

Opportunities Present Themselves

On the 28th of May, 1998, The Government of The Commonwealth of The Bahamas appointed a National Crime Commission. The terms of reference were as follows: "The National Crime Commission was established to identify the main causes of crime in The Bahamas and to make recommendations for the remediation of the same, and to this end the commission held public hearings as was necessary and established procedures for the work of the commission. The commission had to report to the prime minister within six months of appointment."[7]

I was speaking to a group of young people when informed that a representative of the prime minister's office was on the telephone and wished to speak with me. When I was informed that I was appointed to the commission, my heart sank. Yes, I am like many of you in that I also do not like the limelight.

Being on display and moving from my comfort zone is not a welcomed pursuit. Those six months were most interesting for my family and me. I was thrust on a national platform and had both pleasant and unpleasant experiences. My mind, will, and emotions were stretched to unbelievable lengths. What was made visible to me and what I was made visible to has left a permanent mark on my life. I was privileged by having the opportunity of viewing the core of a nation and its people from a unique perspective. The experiences have crystallized God's vision for my life, which includes visibility.

I know what it is like to enter my driveway with my family in the vehicle and see our home sprayed with graffiti death threats. I know the numbness associated with second guessing choices and secretly hoping for life to return to normalcy. In anxious moments, I learned how to pray deep prayers; I learned how to guard my thoughts and the intent of my heart. I learned how to abandon myself and trust an all-powerful and ever-present God. I discovered that visibility is a catalyst for learning. I also know what it is like to hold in confidence national security information and be a part of positive change in a developing nation. There are risks associated with being visible; however, God's grace and wisdom are sufficient.

Most recently in my travels throughout the country, I would see a newly built police station or other facility and smile, knowing that they were a part of our committee's recommendations, or I would see a new policy and recognize it as the outworking of collaborated thoughts and efforts. I have developed a deep love and appreciation for the citizens of my country and a growing passion for their salvation. Comfort is good, but visibility and risks are necessary for purpose realization.

Life is truly as a vapor; by 2006, two members of the appointed Crime Commission had passed into eternity.

It is interesting to note that I was the only member of the Crime Commission that was not from the capital city, Nassau. When God is ready for you, He will draw you from where you are. We are to be visible in our present position and committed to His overall will and purpose for our brief lives; this includes obedience in regard to being visible for all the right reasons and in all seasons.

As you commence this personal study section, be prepared to confess your shortcomings and allow change in your thinking to take place. I encourage you to purchase the book Practical Wisdom for Understanding Your Life when it is released; it is a guide for personal improvement.

Personal Study

Your Life as a Vapor

Session Topic: In this session, you will reexamine areas of your life and complete a research assignment.

Practical Wisdom Discovery

1. State what you believe is presently God's will for your life as it pertains to ministry.
2. Name one major area with which you are struggling. What steps will you take to overcome it?
3. What aspects of a vapor do you see in your life? State how you see them working in your life.
4. How are you responding to The Great Commission Mandate?
5. State your formula for maintaining balance in your personal life and ministry.
6. What Biblical leader do you most identify with and why?

Assignment: Interview at least three leaders in your area. Ask them to explain their concepts of visibility and compare with yours. Share and discuss your finding with a colleague.

Prayer Focus:

- Pray that God will give practical wisdom for developing a balanced life.
- Take time to praise and thank God for your family and personal health.
- Pray for the courage to be visible for the glory of God.

Pray These Scriptures This Week

Psalms 16:11 Proverbs 15:24 John 6:35 Luke 12:23

A Consistent Prayer Life

"Prayer…is the recovery of the soul's breathing."[8] Gerald Heard
The Christian Century

Prayer ought to be as natural and necessary for the Christian leader as breathing. Have you had moments of breathlessness, the collapsing of the chest, the panic that strikes the soul? When the breathing process is inhibited, life painfully slips away. Prayer is our lifeline. Simply put, prayer has been defined as talking with God. It is through this fellowship with God that we receive instruction and guidance. We pray not when we are in trouble or confused, we pray consistently in all seasons of life and ministry. One of the qualities exhibited in a successful Christian leader is a habitual prayer lifestyle. There are many benefits derived from this quality. It is by prayer that we enter a two-way conversation with our creator. Consistent prayer enables our faith to remain strong.

Often, leaders face challenges that seem insurmountable; however, the one to whom we pray and fellowship with is all-wise and powerful. It is in this relationship that we receive the wisdom for the moment; faith soars and the challenge is conquered. We were created for fellowship with God and were given dominion over the earth by our creator; however, when Adam and Eve sinned, man's spirit was separated from God. One of the results of this fallen state is an independent spirit. The fallen spirit often continues to follow the dominion mandate but in its own strength and wisdom. By Jesus we are re-connected to the Godhead, and our dependence on God is acknowledged by not only our need of prayer, but also by the results prayer produces.

As children, our household was full of excitement the night before Christmas. We would ready ourselves and attend as a family our Roman Catholic Parish Church. One particular Christmas when we were teenagers, my brother and I found ourselves sitting in the pew nudging each other throughout the mass, trying to contain our building excitement. You see, as we grew older, the gifts became more sophisticated. We eagerly awaited this new threshold in gift advancement and could hardly wait to open them. We opened our presents immediately when we arrived home just after midnight, discovering that many of them had assembling parts. We never read the instructions and spent hours in utter frustration trying to assemble the parts. Finally, conceding defeat, we looked for the instructions among the trash pile we had created.

Unfortunately, many leaders are in this very state, seeking God among the self-made trash pile as a last-ditch effort. God gives us a vision and a purpose, but He also includes the instructions for its development and fulfillment. The instructions are accessed during and because of prayer. Leaders can spare themselves many unnecessary hardships and disasters if they just maintain a consistent prayer life. A consistent prayer life allows for an unabated flow of information. We are often taught by life's experiences; however, by prayer many truths are caught or received. A healthy relationship with God produces positive spiritual results. God wrote the instructions, and He requires us to read them first and then often. He is even available to help us assemble the parts.

Let God give the challenging vision as we fellowship with Him in a consistent prayerful lifestyle. Let's continually draw nigh to Him for the vision's assembling.

In the epistles, we discover many principles of prayer all pointing in the direction of the requirement of consistent prayer for the

Christian leader. Believers and Christian leaders in particular can only hope to receive knowledge and direction from God by conforming to this type of lifestyle. This is imperative for the success of the leader and organization. Here is one prayer principle in the epistles for our consideration.

Pray Without Ceasing

> "Pray without ceasing. In everything give thanks for this is the will of God in Christ Jesus concerning you." 1 Thessalonians 5:17-18.

Verse 17 of the above Scripture does not mean that we are to be constantly on our knees; that is not possible if we are to fulfill the purposes of life. However, praying without ceasing is attainable. We can and ought to enter into this lifestyle that is actually unbroken fellowship with God. But how is this possible? I call this the *unconscious* aspect of praying.

When you see the word "unconscious," you may think of a prizefighter out for the count or an accident victim in the hospital hooked up to a drip. This is not the intention. The word "unconscious" also means *unaware* and implies an event that is taking place that is not readily recognized or noticed. We are encouraged as leaders to view prayer as *breathing*, or *praying without ceasing*. Let it flow naturally and become a part of your unconscious self. Let me explain this *Practical Wisdom* concept. The unconscious self is the self of which we, at times, are unaware. It is that part of us that habitually performs daily tasks so we can, through our conscious self, learn or attend to new things. Have you ever driven to work or home and wondered how you got there? Your mind was actively focused on another matter and not on the drive. You do not consciously recall stopping at the traffic light or maneuvering around the awkward corner. This is a result of your unconscious self taking over.

Here is another example. In my country, The Bahamas, we have primary and secondary schools; in some other countries they are called elementary and secondary. The truth is that many parents place greater value on the secondary school system. I see this often as a school guidance counselor. Parents are more concerned in enrolling their children in "the best" secondary school. For instance, they will leave their children in an inferior primary school and then spend an enormous amount of funds for seventh through twelfth grades. This choice results in many underachieving students. Please observe:

1. *Primary is not inferior.* To the contrary, primary is the foundation, or what will become the educational unconscious self. It is here that learning skills and concepts becomes habitual. If this foundation is weak or inferior, the educational house we build will be unstable. It will be ineffective for present and future challenges. Potential will not be realized.
2. *Secondary is not superior.* To the contrary, it is what we build upon the primary foundation. If we put new information upon a weak foundation, the cracks will become evident to all. Also, new information can only be evaluated by the primary. A weak primary results in poor or inaccurate evaluations. Lessons and steps missed or wrongly taught in the primary will determine the direction of the secondary. I have seen this as a glaring concern, especially in the discipline of mathematics.

Educational systems that encourage social promotion are equipping students for a lifetime of failure. If the primary is strong and well balanced, the secondary will be clear and successful. Let's view this example in reference to prayer.

Prayer is to be part of our primary foundation grafted into our unconscious self. It ought to get to the place and position in our lives where it flows naturally and as necessary as the breathing process. *Pray without ceasing* is an acquired disposition. You have to work at this until it becomes an unconscious foundation in your life. You have to see this as mandatory in your life and ministry. Your spiritual life depends as much upon this as your natural life depends upon air. The Holy Spirit guides and nudges in this area.

Often, we stress the importance of corporate and designated prayer time. This is fine, needed, and required; however, when we view the prayer life of Jesus, we observe the power of the Holy Spirit in the individual life. Jesus, as the Son of Man, relied on the presence of the Holy Spirit. The Holy Spirit is present in His fullness today, and He dwells within each believer.

He teaches how to pray; He searches the heart of man. If He is within and teaches us, do not overlook the unconscious self as it relates to continual prayer. Jesus remained in constant fellowship with the Father and was always anointed. This lifestyle has been made available for every believer.

Here is a final example. Think of a duck swimming above the water; it appears calm and effortless, but below the water its legs are in full motion. Success often takes place first in the unaware realm, or below the surface. I have observed this trait in many great men and women of God. They might be in conversation and drift to conscious prayer; where did it start? It commenced in the unconscious realm. We are encouraged to stay connected with God; this is possible and necessary for the leader. The successful leader built on the secondary level is due in part to habitual prayer on the primary level.

It has been said that the formula for a miracle is to get the Word of God firstly in your mind, secondly in your heart, and thirdly on your lips. Can this formula work for prayer? I think it can. What is in the heart, the lips will eventually cry and manifest. Make efforts throughout each day and in different circumstances to live out this concept. Give it repeated opportunities to become as natural as breathing.

We are further admonished in verse 18, "In everything give thanks..." Notice not *for* everything, but *in* everything. We are aware that not everything that happens in our personal lives or organizations appears to be good; however, we also know that God is in control, and when we approach our challenges with a thankful heart, we are able to put a positive spin on any circumstance.

Thankfulness releases the miracle-working power of God (See John 6:11). In every situation or circumstance we may find ourselves as leaders, let our heart's response be one of thankfulness. This attitude is a sign of faith in Him who holds the whole world in His hands. God, who called you, is also faithful toward you. So the will of Christ for us is to approach it all with a thankful heart. This is an attitude and action of the primary foundation.

If you complain of the state you are in or about what is taking place, you will never see the possible change, growth, understanding, or deliverance from God's view. Often, God gives us the test first, and then He explains the lesson. We have the Holy Spirit to guide us in this area.

The Holy Spirit's Guidance

Some time back I was invited as a speaker for a function in New York City; this was about a year after the 9/11 tragedy. My flight itinerary required travel through two airports, and by the time we arrived in NYC, I was quite upset with the manner of body and bag searches endured at the airports in route. When I arrived at the hotel and checked into my room on the fifty-third floor, the Holy Spirit summoned me to the window and urged me to look down onto the street. The pedestrians below appeared as ants traveling in all directions; however, there was an order in it all. There were well-defined lines and an unconscious system. God gently rebuked and invited me to see life from His vantage point.

When you sit, stand, or walk with God, you see beyond your challenges and view the possibilities for success. Did the body and bag searches cease? No, they continued for fifteen more consecutive trips to the USA. What did change was my attitude.

Finally, one day when clearing a checkpoint in Florida, the security said "You are a minister. Come through." The lesson was learnt and the tide turned. This was in part to me developing the primary foundation of praying without ceasing and maintaining a thankful attitude. Nothing can take the place of the Holy Spirit's guidance that we receive and is intimately ours by staying connected to God in prayer.

"And when he is come, he will reprove the world of sin, and of righteousness, and of judgment" (John 16:8). Let's adapt this Scripture to building your vision. The Holy Spirit helps the leader answer the following:

- *Is there any sin in my life as the leader that will hinder the fulfillment of the vision?* The Holy Spirit will answer this question with clarity.
- *What is the right thing (rightwiseness) to do in regard to the vision?* We all have our plans and views on how the vision should be accomplished. What matters in the end is only God's will. The Holy Spirit teaches us and reveals the will of the Godhead.
- *What is God's judgment on my attitudes, actions, or vision steps?* We want to know if we are pleasing God. The Holy Spirit answers these questions.

Prayer is vital to our success as leaders. It is a lifeline that must be obtained and maintained. It is a spiritual filter that purifies our motives and actions. Vision is birthed and fulfilled in part because of sustained prayer. Character is molded as a result of obeying the promptings received in prayer. Miracles are secured by prayers of faith, and hearts are warmed by the fellowship derived from prayer.

Many leaders claim that they are too busy to pray. Are they too busy to breathe? This personal study section will assist you in refocusing on the value and practice of praying.

Personal Study

A Consistent Prayer Life

Session Topic: In this session, you will review the concepts of prayer as presented by the author.

Practical Wisdom Discovery

1. List at least two reasons why prayer is a must for a leader.
2. Explain the unconscious self as it relates to prayer.
3. What does the author imply by the word "secondary"?
4. Why is the concept of primary foundation important to prayer?
5. What value is there in having a thankful heart?
6. Develop a prayer journal for a week, noting the practicing of daily unconscious prayer. List your observations.

Assignment: Read the Book of Acts and make a list showing the values of prayer.

Prayer Focus:

- Pray for those who are praying for you and your ministry.
- Take time to praise and thank God that you are hidden in Him.
- Commit to developing a more consistent prayer life.

Pray These Scriptures This Week

Psalms 119:130 Galatians 2:20 Philippians 3:13 Proverbs 4:20-23

Seek and Give Counsel

It is necessary for the Christian leader to seek godly counsel. Leadership is a life changing and challenging journey and the counsel of others is vital for destination realization. Equally vital is the responsibility as a leader to give counsel to others.

Leaders interact with numerous people and for any number of reasons; however, there are special persons needed in a leader's life who will help ensure personal and organizational success. In this chapter, you will find *Practical Wisdom* principles as they relate to three types of persons that you will need in your life at each level of ministry and/or personal development. The three types of persons are:

- A Barnabas
- A Timothy
- An Epaphroditus

Barnabas

> Who, when he came, and had seen the grace of God, was glad, and exhorted them all, that with purpose of heart they would cleave unto the Lord. For he was a good man, and full of the Holy Ghost and of faith…Acts 11:23, 24

The Christian leader Barnabas was an encourager. You have to be connected to an encourager. Your Barnabas will help you see the glass half-full as opposed to half-empty. When plans fail or unexpected challenges arise, your Barnabas will speak words of life to you. Usually, you will find that this person is often older than you and has traveled the road on which you are presently. However, at times God will send a younger Barnabas your way. Typically, a Barnabas is a person with insight beyond his years and a high level of spiritual maturity. Our Scriptures show that a biblical-model Barnabas will:

- *Encourage you to remain true to God and His call upon your life.* He will never encourage you to abandon the call of God.

- *Encourage you to remain true with all your heart.* His words will help you remain focused and motivated. It is so easy to lose your drive because of the challenges and stress associated with leadership. Your Barnabas will encourage you to finish as strong as you started.

- *Be a good person.* Your Barnabas will have a good report of those within and without the church. He is a good person, reflected in his conduct, commitment, and conversation. Your Barnabas must be a true role model—an ambassador for Christ.

- *Be full of the Holy Spirit and faith.* He is Spirit-led, therefore his words bring life; faith-driven, therefore his life produces results. He has to demonstrate the essence of a spirit-led life.

It is important to note that you may have different persons fulfilling this role at various times in your development. Some people will outgrow you, and some you will outgrow. People may change; however, the need for a Barnabas will remain consistent. As you continue to develop as a leader, it may very well be necessary to repeatedly seek out a Barnabas-type.

Timothy

> Paul, an apostle of Jesus Christ by the will of God, according to the promise of life which is in Christ Jesus. To Timothy, my dearly beloved son: Grace, mercy, and peace, from God the Father and Christ Jesus our Lord. I thank God, whom I serve from my forefathers with pure conscience, that without ceasing I have remembrance of thee in my prayers night and day; Greatly desiring to see thee, being mindful of thy tears, that I may be filled with joy; When I recall to remembrance the unfeigned faith that is in thee, which dwelt first in thy grandmother Lois, and thy mother Eunice; and I am persuaded that is in thee also. Wherefore I put thee in remembrance that thou stir up the gift of God, which is in thee by the putting on of my hands. 2 Timothy 1:1-6

Timothy was the apostle Paul's son in the ministry. It is important to be an encourager. A wise, elderly missionary once told me that whatever you give away belongs to you twice. I asked for an explanation. He went on to explain that when you invest in the life of another, you see your gift not only in your life, but in theirs; therefore it is twice yours. Every Paul should have a ministry son, and the relationship should naturally develop into a mentoring process. From the quoted Scriptures, we see that a biblical-model Paul will:

- Identify with a protégé.
- Thank God for and remember their Timothy in prayer continually.
- Be emotionally attached. Desiring to spend quality time in mentoring and fellowship.
- Know the immediate family and discern spiritual traits.
- Encourage the stirring of gifts. He will challenge his protégé to maximize his potential.

- Acknowledge his role in his Timothy's spiritual life and gift development. He has a hand in his life and ministry.

I believe that the greatest ministry a person will have is that of mentoring. It is important to build great organizations and ministries but greater to assist in building great people. We ought to have a positive influence on as many people as possible. It need not be a lifetime of mentoring; it may simply be a season. Timothy types will constantly crisscross your path: be willing and prepared to mentor some of them.

Epaphroditus

> Yet I supposed it necessary to send to you Epaphroditus, my brother, and companion in labour, and fellow soldier, but your messenger, and he that ministered to my wants. For he longed after you all, and was full of heaviness, because that ye had heard that he had been sick. For indeed he was sick nigh unto death: but God had mercy on him; and not on him only, but on me also, lest I should have sorrow upon sorrow. I sent him therefore the more carefully, that, when ye see him again, ye may rejoice, and that I may be the less sorrowful. Receive him therefore in the Lord with all gladness; and hold such in reputation: Because for the work of Christ he was nigh unto death, not regarding his life, to supply your lack of service toward me. Philippians 2:25-30

Every leader must have a friend with whom he can look across the table and share his heart. Epaphroditus was this kind of friend. Paul calls him a brother. Leadership is quite difficult at times, especially when you are in transitional phases and shifting from one scope of ministry and embracing another. Shifts will take their toll on a leader. You cannot expect personal counsel from those you serve, and it's at these moments that you comprehend the importance of and desire the companionship of a brother.

Do you have that kind of friend, a person with whom you may share your fears, dreams, and failures? Every leader needs a godly friend. Let's take a closer look at Epaphroditus:

- He was a brother, companion, and fellow soldier in the ministry. What allowed their relationship to be close was the common ground they shared. They had similar convictions and godly desires. They had the ability to sharpen each other. They walked parallel paths.

- He was there for Paul. Paul states, "He ministered to my wants." Friends are like medicine; they provide a healing touch. They give of themselves for their friends. Paul had wants in the form of personal needs, and his friend was there and provided comfort, companionship, and service.

- As a friend, he neglected his own sickness for the betterment of his friend.

- As a faithful friend of a leader, others were instructed to hold him in high esteem. Being a friend of a leader requires a special quality. Leaders, it would appear partly because of their visibility and transparency, have few friends.

- Epaphroditus jeopardized his own ministry and risked his life to serve a friend. His actions were love-advancement of the work of Christ motivated.

God knits us with others, and sometimes the relationship develops into a meaningful friendship. These friendships endure the test of time and trials. I have found that some of my Barnabas-types have developed into lifelong friends. These three types are vital to your development and success.

Let us now take a look at the value of a mentor and coach. Mentors and coaches may have to be hired and their time honored by you.

There Is Value in Having A Mentor and Coach

Every Christian leader ought to have a mentor and coach. Having a mentor or coach who is able to speak into your life is a real blessing. Not every leader of your covering will be a mentor or coach. A mentor will have the ability and time to pour into your life from his or her own experiences. A coach will assist in drawing out of you the gifts placed there by the Holy Spirit.

As you seek godly advice, stay open for the Holy Spirit's connection with a mentor or coach. I have found that often it is not someone you expect. A mentor and coach may not stay with you for the long haul; often they are transitional in your life and endeavors. 1 Thessalonians 2:8 gives a brief, concise look at the heart of a mentor and spiritual coach. "We loved you so much that we were delighted to share with you not only the gospel of God but our lives as well"(Paraphrased). This is the attitude of a mentor and coach. They are willing to expose themselves and teach by example. They not only share the Word of God, but their lives as well.

I am grateful to the Godhead for my spiritual mentor. My mentor and friend, Pastor Ernie DeLoach, uncovered not only the Words of Life but opened his heart and home. Truly in those formative years of personal and leadership development, I had the opportunity to watch and learn from a seasoned minister. This mentoring relationship has continued for more than twenty-five years. Throughout the years I've learned the value of prayer from him and understand the importance of being a people's person by watching his interaction with others and noting the results. I witnessed the power of compassion through my association with him and observed godly character and Christ-likeness in him.

Today, I keenly make a note of how he gracefully adjusts to his cycles of life and ministry and marvel at his steadfastness in the call and faithfulness toward his God.

You may, at times, require a mentor and coach who is an expert in a particular area. It might be administrative, managerial, goal setting, etc. This interaction may be needed and required for promotion to the next level. In the corporate world, it is called "executive coaching" and is normally sought out and secured for employees climbing the leadership ladder. The Christian leader ought also to take full advantage of this service and process.

Personal Study

Seek and Give Counsel

Session Topic: In this session, you will review the importance of counsel.

Practical Wisdom Discovery

1. Name the three types of persons that a leader will need at each level. Give one reason for each type.
2. Who are your current Barnabas, Timothy, and Epaphroditus?
3. What value is there in having a mentor?
4. What value is there in being a mentor?
5. Explain Paul's relationship to Timothy?
6. Explain the impact a mentor has had on your life and ministry.

Assignment: Research the ministry of mentoring and evaluate whether a mentoring ministry is feasible for your leadership team. Give reasons for your conclusions.

Prayer Focus:

- Pray for the other Christian leaders in your area.
- Pray for your leadership team.
- Commit to becoming a better role model.

Pray These Scriptures This Week

Proverbs 3:30   Romans 13:7   Romans 12:18   Proverbs 3:27

The Courage to Walk by Faith

"For they conquer who believe they can."[9] Virgil

The Bible has a great deal to say about the subject of faith; however, the definition of faith is recorded in only one place in the Bible.

"Now faith is the substance of things hoped for, the evidence of things not seen" (Hebrews 11:1). Verse 6 states the importance of faith, "But, without faith it is impossible to please him, for he that cometh to God must believe that he is, and that he is a rewarder of them that diligently seek him."

Faith understands two different kinds of reality:

1. Faith is concerned with things that are future. I believe this aspect of faith is reaching into the future, seeing the purpose of God, and pulling that purpose into the present. By faith, we declare God's vision for the organization, and without faith, we cannot please God.
2. Faith knows that the future is real, that things unseen do exist. We walk by faith and not by sight. Faith believes in what God says, not in what is or is not seen naturally.

When my wife and I purchased our home and ministry base in The Bahamas, the former owner explained that beneath the overgrown brush on the four-acre site was a winding concrete pathway. This pathway, he said, extended throughout the entire property. Recognizing our puzzled expression, he quickly added, "Trust me, it is really there, for I built it myself." Those words often echo in my mind and spirit. God is the architect of our future. He does not create the future when we arrive there. It already exists by faith. There is a winding concrete pathway beneath the brush. We are to walk by faith and not by sight. Faith sees what God saw, faith speaks what God spoke. Faith trusts the testimony of God.

Trusting your life and making a full commitment to God is faith; therefore faith is more than a mindset or attribute; faith is a personal relationship with God. This relationship determines the priorities of one's life. This relationship is one of love, built on trust and dependence. Faith is having a total dependence upon God. Here are some *Practical Wisdom* principles that relate to our faith walk: It is never easy to fulfill a God-given mandate. It takes a well-designed plan, courage, and faith.

The workplace ministry leader Nehemiah discovered this as he answered the call of God to return to Jerusalem and rebuild the wall of the city that was in ruin. Nehemiah had a plan, but a plan alone will never accomplish the mission of the vision. The best-designed plan should be in the hands of a faith-led leader. Nehemiah was this kind of a leader.

Nehemiah, after receiving the vision, remained faithful at his job performing his daily duties and enjoyed the favor of the King Artaxerxes, his boss. He waited on God's timing. I believe waiting takes more faith than ill-conceived, rushed actions (See Nehemiah 2:1-9). When the time was right, Nehemiah, exercising godly wisdom, asked for a letter of permission to carry out his God-given mandate. By asking for a permission letter, Nehemiah was using the favor of the king as an instrument, or rebuilding tool. It also gave him the authority to move freely as he secured the needed materials.

A good leader anticipates upcoming challenges and plans ahead, seizing opportunities of influence. This favor would provide a much-needed wall of resistance in the face of opposition.

Opposition to Nehemiah's vision came as anticipated. Sanballat the Horonite and Tobiah the Ammonite tried to destroy the efforts to rebuild the wall. Nehemiah, however, succeeded in the undertaking because he had well planned his moves and had strong, unwavering faith. He was courageous enough to walk by faith and not by sight (See Nehemiah 2:7-10).

Nehemiah understood some important *Practical Wisdom* principles of vision casting and vision completion. Among them are the following:

- *Move forward with a plan.* It is better to have a plan and let God change it than having no plan at all. Many organizations fail simply because they fail to plan. Nehemiah knew there would be obstacles, and altering of the plan might be possible; however, he was compelled to move forward. Plan your work, and then work your plan with an eye fixed on the future and an ear bent toward the voice of the Holy Spirit.

- *Move forward by faith*, but realize that people of faith have orderly minds. Faith is not haphazard thinking. Faith-led leaders understand the risks involved. They further understand and appreciate that hard work may be involved in fulfilling a vision. Faith-led leaders know that sometimes there is a *blind leap* of faith, but they also know this is not the normal way; however, when it does happen, they know that God is at the end of that calculated leap.

- *Be prepared spiritually for opposition.* If no one opposes you, chances are the vision is not from the Lord. Opposition will come. It is not personal; we wrestle not against flesh and blood (See Ephesians 6:12). Our opposition is spiritual. If you are a sleeping giant, your opposition will not wake you. If you are an awakened giant, your opposition will attempt to put you to sleep. Opposition may come in many forms. Be prepared and constantly look to the Lord for strength and guidance.

- *Know when to consult and when not to.* Talking to the wrong people even in the right time will hinder the vision. Likewise, talking to the right people in the wrong time will also spell defeat. Nehemiah inspected the wall at night and alone. He did his homework first. When his steps were organized, he shared the vision and plan for rebuilding the wall. His consultation was limited and purposefully directed.

- *God gives us favor with those in authority.* Use this favor to fulfill the God-given vision, not selfish desires. Favor is like grace; we do not deserve it, and it is unlimited in respect to the vision. If we take care of the God-given vision, God will take care of us. Often, favor is for a season, not for the building of lifelong alliances. So, do not procrastinate—move in faith and favor when God bids you.

- *Pray often and listen more.* Prayer is a sustaining exercise. It becomes necessary for leaders to pray often. Developing a lifestyle of prayer is a top priority. I find that in this phase of the vision it is even more important to exercise the part of prayer called "listening." Listen for God's voice and direction. Listen with your inner ear. When you hear, obey fully.

- *Build a team.* You cannot do it alone. Groups of families make a great team. Nehemiah used families to rebuild the portion of the wall connected to their sphere of influence and responsibility. The team built and provided protection at the same time. It is important to build a solid team, and families are a vital part of that team; however, do not limit yourself to any one group. Nehemiah himself was the only representative of his family. Please do not overemphasize the value of teams. There are aspects to the fulfillment of a vision that only a leader can do.

A challenging vision builds faith in the lives of all involved. Faith becomes one of the foundational attributes of the organization. A faith-inspired and God-led organization plans and develops those plans while trusting God each step of the way.

The Power of the Holy Spirit Is Evident In This Kind of Leader and Organization

"Now unto him that is able to do exceeding abundantly above all that we ask or think, according to the power that worketh in us." Ephesians 3:20

The Triune God works in us through the ministry of the Holy Spirit. We accomplish the challenging vision in His power. A challenging vision forces a total dependency upon the Lord, and the result is a greater level of a faith walk.

The Holy Spirit is called the Comforter. This term comes from the word *Parakletos,*[10] which literally means "called to one's side or one's aid." *Parakletos* is primarily a verbal adjective, and the word generally suggests the capability or adaptability for giving aid. In Jesus' day, it was used in a court of justice to denote a legal assistant or counsel for the defense; in essence, it meant an advocate. Jesus Christ was this to His disciples and said the Holy Spirit would be this to us.

Prior to entering fulltime ministry, I was employed as a shipping agent. One of my duties was facilitating Customs and Immigration officers in the clearing of oil tankers, cruise liners, and cargo vessels. As we waited to board, it was fascinating to watch a tugboat come alongside of the vessel and proceed to berth it at an oil jetty or dock. It took a great deal of trust for the captain to relinquish control of his bridge to the tugboat pilot. This massive force was now in the control of a seemly inferior and almost invisible entity. Faith is welcoming the Holy Spirit alongside and relinquishing control to Him. Let His power work unabated in your life and organization. The writer of Hebrews admonishes us to walk by faith.

> Let us therefore fear, least, a promise being left us of entering into his rest, any of you should seem to come short of it. For unto us was the gospel preached, as well as unto them: but the word preached did not profit them, not being mixed with faith in them that heard it. Hebrews 4:1-2

As we hear the Word of God for our lives, we are to mix it with faith and walk in obedience to what we have heard. The same principle is true for the receiving of a vision. It is God's Word or purpose for the organization and us. We are to lay hold of it and walk by faith. That is walking not by what we see in the natural, but by what God desires for us. The Word not mixed with faith will produce no vision realization.

ANOTHER OLD TESTAMENT LEADERSHIP EXAMPLE

When the Lord rose up Joshua to lead the children of Israel into the Promised Land, he instructed Joshua to be strong and very courageous. This instruction was repeated twice, as it were to indicate alike the inward courage of faith and the outward courage of deed. This instruction holds true for us today. It takes faith to believe God for the vision. It takes courage to live out the vision. There is no other way around it. Without faith, it is impossible to please God. It takes faith to look beyond our insecurities and boldly go where we have never been before, completing what we never dreamed of doing.

It is important to note that the assignment given to Joshua was not out of his area of training. The conquest of the Promised Land was a military venture, and Joshua was indeed a military commander. However, the dynamics had changed; instead of receiving orders from Moses, the command was now Joshua's, and he would now give the orders. The decision-making process was now his. He moved from being a receiver to a giver. Nothing would happen unless he gave the command, and the responsibility for the outcome would be on his shoulders. He had to articulate God wishes. This takes a great measure of courage.

Joshua was now out of his comfort zone. As one trained in the military, he knew that his army would obey his command; they might question him inwardly but never outwardly. They understood the rules that govern the army and had conformed to that mindset. However, he now had to lead the religious and civilian sectors.

Joshua knew firsthand of the challenges that Moses faced with the religious and civil groups. They marched by a different drumbeat. They were often quick to complain and challenge the leadership. He also knew how the people loved Moses; would he find respect and loyalty toward him? God had already told him to take them all safely across, so a division in the camp was not an option. This called for a fresh courage, renewed strength, and an unwaving trust in the Lord.

God uses our preparation and gifts; however, we have to be courageous in the stretching process. God admonishes His new leader, Joshua, and gives him some vital instructions and promises. God told him to have courage, and He would provide the wisdom through His Word. That is an unbeatable combination. A careful study of Joshua 1 reveals the following:

1. *Transferal of the mandate to complete the work started by Moses to Joshua is completed.* The leader changed; however, the vision remained the same. I believe that we have been so vision-programmed that we think everyone must have an original vision from the Lord. Here is an example to the contrary. God did not change the vision, He replaced the leader. Joshua's style would be different; challenges would shift, but the vision was the same: finish what Moses started.

2. My wife and I pastored a church for eleven years. After nine years, God identified our replacement, and I poured my efforts into him. One day in conversation, he said, "Pastor, my vision for this ministry is to complete the vision God gave to you." I thought at the time this displayed keen sensitivity to the things

of God and took great courage. To accept a call to an existing ministry is a wonderful opportunity and privilege. Do not, in haste, change the vision. Seek the Lord first. The Lord will ask some of us to build upon the foundation of another, even if it is only for a season. Build with courage, integrity, and grace.

3. *The mandate required him to move forward with all the people.* This is always a challenging command. Jesus received such a command and reported to the Father that He kept all entrusted to Him but Judas. It is easy to love those who love you. It is almost impossible to lead those who hate or constantly oppose you. We are called to reach and teach people with various temperaments. It is not optional; you will have difficulty accepting some folk. However, peculiar as they are, they are God's handiwork. Helping them cross over is our mandate. I believe this is the thought attached to The Great Commission, all nations, and people groups. We have tried to become spiritual specialists, working with those we feel gifted to help. The command given to Joshua was to bring them all across. The gifted and ungifted, the strong and weak, the rich and poor, the good and bad, the young and old, the married and single, you get the picture, don't you? No wonder Joshua needed courage.

4. *What God promised to Moses is transferred to Joshua.* This is an important point. The vision is transferable. The blessings are also transferable. It is important for leaders and those they lead to understand this *Practical Wisdom* principle: "The promises of God are transferable." Sometimes we even reap where others have sown. Leaders are to partake of the promises of the Lord. The new leader not only inherits the problems but the promises also. If he has the challenge, he has the blessings.

5. *God assured him that no one could defeat him.* God announced to Joshua that he would have to fight, but he would win them all. What a confidence booster. Jesus said He would build His

Church and the gates of hell would not prevail against it (See Matthew 16:18). If the vision is from the Lord, the victory will manifest itself. Where there is a vision, there is also provision.

6. *God assured him that he would be with him.* (1) It is a comfort to know that God would stay connected. He does not send us and not accompany us. Jesus told His disciples that He would go, but the Comforter would come, and in fact, they would be better off for it. God walks with us in the battles, through the floods, and into the Promised Land. I am sure Joshua remembered the times when God showed up for Moses; he now had this same assurance. It might not be a burning bush experience or a mountaintop experience, but God would be there. (2) *Not fail him.* Joshua received this declaration. God never fails. His timing is always right. His wisdom is heaven sent. His promises are true forevermore. His counsel is sure. His weapons are mighty. (3) *Never forsake him.* This is similar to not failing him. Have you been in a battle for your life, needed a friend to stand up for you, and that friend bailed? Have you ever been in a fiery furnace and felt abandoned? God promised Joshua that He would never turn His back on him. King David said he never saw the righteous forsaken or his seed begging bread (Psalm 37:25). God made a comforting commitment to Joshua. Every leader that moves forward in God's will receives the same commitment from the Lord.

7. *God instructed Joshua to keep the law of God.* Obedience to God's Word would make his steps prosperous. Joshua's prosperity was wrapped up in keeping God's law. God's will is contained in His Word. Joshua was to be guided by the map of God's Word. This is the Word that Moses recorded, and even though it is today Old Covenant, or Old Wine, it was God's Word of the day. It spoke to every area of concern and laid out the precepts of Almighty God. Joshua walked in this Word, and his walk enabled

> him to enter the Promised Land. When tempted by Satan, Jesus responded, "...It is written, man shall not live by bread alone, but by every word that proceedeth out of the mouth of God" (Matthew 4:4).

Nehemiah and Joshua were courageous leaders. They walked with God and fulfilled their purposes. Their examples teach us much about the values of godly leadership and the power of an eternal God. Let us be encouraged and learn by their examples. Enter your personal study section with this in focus.

Personal Study

The Courage to Walk by Faith

Session Topic: In this session, you will review the leadership styles of Nehemiah and Joshua.

Practical Wisdom Discovery

1. How did Nehemiah approach his ministry assignment? What principles from his approach can you incorporate in your vision-building efforts?
2. Why is faith important to vision building? Give reasons.
3. Compare the leadership styles of Nehemiah and Joshua. Make a chart and list them.
4. List the instructions God gave Joshua and briefly state their importance.
5. What aspect of leadership do you find most difficult and why?
6. What are your views on building on another minister's foundation?

Assignment: Interview at least two leaders and ask them what role faith plays in their organizations. Record and discuss your findings.

Prayer Focus:

- Pray for those who are in leadership positions.
- Take time to praise and thank God for the organizations in your area.
- Commit to walk by faith in all areas of your life.
- Ask God to help you design a plan for your ministry.

Pray These Scriptures This Week

Acts 4:10, 13, 21 Acts 5:12 Acts 4:29-31 Acts 6:3, 10

Wines and Wineskins

> "When two truths seem to directly oppose each other, we must not question either, but remember there is a third—God—who reserves to Himself the right to harmonize them."[11] Madam Anne Soymanov Swetchine

In recent years, much has been communicated about the subject of new wine and new wineskins. Wine and wineskins have come to represent (1) forms of church or organizational governments, (2) former and current moves of God, and (3) shifts in vision. There are some excellent books on the market that cover these aspects in their entirety. It is my intent to present what ought to be the obvious: that vision is greatly influenced by the form or structures it is connected to, or that your choice of governmental structure impacts vision casting and building. I wish to offer a few *Practical Wisdom* suggestions for leaders who may find themselves in either of the two major forms of church government, which I believe to be democratic and apostolic. For those who are in transition, this chapter may answer some of your questions. Transitional ministry shifts are becoming more frequent in the Body of Christ and may be complex. In the *Building Your Vision* workshop, this subject is covered and our consultation services are designed for seeing a leader-ministry through these often uncharted waters.

Understanding the Wine and Wineskin Principles

Old Covenant to New Covenant. The Old Covenant pointed forward to the New Covenant. John the Baptist was the last of the Old Covenant, or Testament Prophets, and was assigned the mission of preparing the way for the Lord Jesus Christ, the establisher of the New Covenant.

John the Baptist preached repentance and declared the Kingdom of Heaven is at hand (Matthew 3:1-2). This prophet stated that he was not worthy to carry the shoes of Jesus (Matthew 3:11). This statement indicates that John was fully aware of his role as the forerunner of Jesus and gracefully and consistently labored in that purpose.

John's Disciples Ask for Clarification

I believe one of the most difficult seasons in any organization, ministry, or leader's life is the period called "transition," or evolution. Change makes people uncomfortable and often results in comparisons. Transition brings with it a unique protocol. Notice the following:

As Jesus was increasing in popularity, John was decreasing. This was by divine design; John was Old Covenant, and Jesus was New Covenant. The purposes and promises of each covenant were different. John the Baptist's disciples wanted an explanation on why the two camps had differing philosophies regarding food, fasting, and prayer, so they questioned Jesus as to why John had them fasting and praying often, but He allowed His disciples to eat and enjoy themselves. John's disciples did not spiritually perceive what John knew as destiny. Jesus responds in Matthew 9:15-17.

> ...Can the children of the bride chamber mourn, as long as the bridegroom is with them? But the days will come, when the bridegroom shall be taken away from them, and then shall they fast. No man putteth a piece of new cloth unto an old garment, for that which is put in to fill it up taketh from the garment, and

> the rent is made worse. Neither do men put new wine into old bottles: else the bottles break, and the wine runneth out, and the bottles perish: but they put new wine into new bottles, and both are preserved.

Let's observe the following:

- *There is a time and season for everything.* The purpose for the season and the structure employed will often predetermine the actions that follow. This is true in our personal lives as well as in our organizations. The purpose of God for John determined his mindset and actions. This is one of the reasons why we must not allow tradition or what has become the norm to determine our priorities. What we wish to see as permanent might be transitional. John was the forerunner, his mission was divine, but it was expendable in that it had a starting and finishing point. Many missions God bids us to undertake have a winding-up point, and often ministries within an organization have an identifiable lifespan. As a leader, you must be able to differentiate when to continue or discontinue a structure, ministry, or program. Often, we wish to keep at the forefront the forerunner and never move forward in God's vision.
- *If you love the old cloth and the old wineskin, you will not attach the new to it.* Everything that is old was once new. The attachment of the new to the old will degrade the value of the old. Because God is replacing a structure or enhancing a message does not mean that what is being replaced or enhanced has depreciated value. However, if you attempt to mix, blend, repair, or fill the old with the new, you will create severe damage. Refraining from attaching both is actually a display of love for the old. In the overall scheme, the old retains its place of significance. Leaders leave organizations

and fellowships for numerous reasons. Here we are given a noble one. Attempting to remain in a structure that was not designed to support new wine will eventually destroy the old wineskin. So love, appreciation, and obedience are compelling factors for moving forward. Many have stayed in old wineskin structures and agitated for change from within. In light of the quoted Scripture, how successful do you think this method is?

- *If the old is destroyed because of the new, the new will also perish.* How is this possible? God moves forward with His plans and seasons. Those experiencing the new wine will want to propagate the new wine message. This is natural; however, when this transpires within the framework of the old wineskin structure, confusion and divisions may occur. This can and often will undermine the structural integrity of the organization; unnecessary comparisons, debates, schisms, and challenges emerge. What was intended for good is misunderstood, suspiciously and negatively received, and now has the momentum required for the destruction of the old wineskin and the new wine. The safeguarding of the organization's constitution and by-laws often becomes the focal point, and the new wine move of God is missed. This is unfortunate but is happening within numerous organizations and churches.

- *New stuff into new stuff, please.* John the Baptist and his disciples were the old guard. John was the forerunner, preparing the way for Jesus. His mission was clear to him, and as the last great representative of the Old Covenant, he had the responsibility and privilege to declare, "...Behold the lamb of God, which taketh away the sin of the world" (John 1:29). Through Jesus, a New Covenant was established, and it demanded a mindset shift, a shift that would produce greater works. The old pointed toward the new; however, Jesus declared that the greatest of the old would not be greater than the least of the new (Matthew 11:11). This Scripture has great importance as it relates to vision. "Verily I say unto you, Among them that are born of women there hath not risen a greater than John the Baptist: notwithstanding he that is least in the Kingdom of heaven is greater than he." John was born under the Old Covenant. The least person in the Kingdom of Heaven manifested on the earth born under the New Covenant is greater than John. How can this be? It appears the emphasis is not on the person or persons but on the covenants. John represents Old Covenant, or Old Wineskins, and his message represents old wine. This is only so because Jesus represents New Covenant, or New Wineskins, and his message represents new wine. Until Jesus arrived and established the New Covenant, John and his message represented new wineskins and new wine. If a person embraces the mandate of the Kingdom of Heaven and walks in Kingdom principles, although that person may seem unimportant or insignificant, he will achieve great things, and this is a result of the New Covenant. What an astonishing declaration. There is value in the old but destiny in the new. The structure and the message (vision) determine God-given possibilities.

Vision and Governmental Structures

One of the greatest challenges for any visionary is the ability to attract or develop ministry and leadership teams. With varying forms of church or organizational governments, this task is more difficult than it first appears.

One philosophy is that leaders cast the vision, while another is that a team-members cast vision. Some advocate that the vision is board-led, while others prescribe to a leader-led view. *Can two walk together, except they be agreed?* (Amos 3:3). As children, we played numerous games during the summer months. The one that provided the most fun and laughter was the three-legged race. Participants were paired off and had one leg each tied to their partner's. In order to succeed, the team would have to agree on a strategy. They had to run in agreement. Many visions are suspended or aborted because of the inability to agree firstly on the wineskin structure. A double-minded *organization* is unstable in all *its* ways (James 1:8, emphasis mine), and secondly a lack of operating in an agreed structure.

Peter Wagner, in his book, *Changing Church*, presents an outline of what the average local church level of government looks like. Here is his assessment.

On the local church level, there are five general assumptions concerning the role of the pastor in the old denominational wineskins:

1. Pastors are employees of the church.
2. Pastors can come and go. The average pastoral tenure among Southern Baptist, for example, is less than three years.
3. Pastors are the enablers. Their responsibility is to implement the vision of the congregation.
4. Pastors are the "medicine men" of the church rather than the "tribal chiefs." They are expected to do religious things but not to lead.
5. Pastors are subject to performance reviews. They can be fired at will.

In contrast, apostolic churches make a different set of assumptions concerning the local church pastor.

1. Pastors—not the congregations—cast the vision.
2. Pastors major in leadership and minor in management.
3. Pastors make top-drawer policy decisions and delegate the rest.
4. Pastors build a solid management team of both elders and staff.

Pastors are not subject to the authority of this team, but the team serves at the pleasure of the pastors. Staff members are employees of their pastor, not of the church.

5. Pastors are called for life.
6. Pastors choose their successors.[12]

This comparison is an eye opener and reinforces the need to clearly understand one's organizational structure. I am sure there are groups in either camp that have developed some measure of flexibility; however, the above comparison represents the norm.

My First Assignment

My first assignment as a minister was that of a circuit minister for five small congregations on a family island in The Bahamas. Like every inexperienced preacher, I was determined to accomplish what no one before me did. I quickly discovered that others were stakeholders in the future of the churches and rightly so. As I became more acquainted with the organizational and functional structures of the churches, I concluded that I was placed in a peculiar position.

The churches, like many others, were deacon and membership led. This may be called democratic leadership, where votes determine who leads and the thrust of the church or organization. The five churches on that island had seen pastors come and go and eventually developed the attitude that they were just a training ground for inexperienced leaders. We were welcomed with a polite "let's wait and see if they stay" attitude. My wife and I had left our jobs and the comfort of city living and were second guessing our decision. We knew that we were called to ministry, but the structure and current situation of the churches made us feel uneasy to say the least.

I thank God for the leader of the fellowship at that time. He had traveled the road we were on and was an insightful man of God. His counsel galvanized the following concepts in my mind and heart:

- I was walking into a situation that probably would be transitional. Therefore I should understand my contribution to the overall plan of God for the organization and area.

- I would be best served to wait on my ministry by serving in the areas of my gifts. God had given me a vision that was future focused; however, seeing His mission for me at this stage would prove beneficial for all.

- I needed to develop local leaders with the view that one day a local leader would occupy my place and role of leadership.

- I must continue to develop skills as a leader and remain teachable and pliable in the hands of God.

- What my hands found to do for the Lord, I must do with a full commitment.

My wife and I ministered on that island for exactly four years and enjoyed a fruitful season of ministry. As I look back now, those five churches provided partial training ground for what I do today. There is a vision for your life and a number of missions along the way. I wish to now offer suggestions on how to build a vision for the organizational view *that vision is cast by the leader.*

Stages of a Vision

The Personal Vision is the vision of the leader. The Lord provides the leader with a vision. This vision can be drawn from many areas. The vision can be a combination of what the leader has received from the Lord in prayer, experienced, observed in the community as a pressing need, or received as input from others. It all becomes a reflection of the personal grid of the leader. It contains the leader's working out of the plan of the Lord for the organization.

This vision also contains the fears, personal hopes, and dreams of the visionary. It is important to stress this. Many leaders allow these personal needs to denominate their thinking and planning processes. If the vision remains at this level, God's plan for the organization will never be truly realized, and the vision, over time may only become self-serving for the leader.

The vision will remain in the realm of the leader's personal grid and normally dies with him. The final vision product is intended to be greater in scope than any one person's perspective. The personal vision is the seed so to speak, not the tree and its fruit. The fruit is contained in this vision seed; however, it requires other factors for growth and full maturity.

The Team Vision is the vision of the appointed or elected leadership team, plus or minus the members of the organization and the leader. It is an established fact that members of leadership teams have their own view as to the way forward for an organization. With differing temperaments and gifts, this ought to be viewed as positive not negative. This is not a challenge of the vision you declared as a leader; however, it's a search for the right mission or missions needed to fulfill the vision. Do you recall this statement presented at the beginning of the book?

> Throughout this book, you ought to interpret the reference to vision as a vision complete with a mission statement, major areas of focus, and well-defined action steps. A complete vision is biblical, future oriented, directional, and functional.

The Team Vision Level is intended to be the catalyst used to begin the process of developing the complete vision. The leader and the team are starting to dialogue on how to construct the complete vision. The catchword here is "flexibility." All parties concerned must be pliable in the hands of the Holy Spirit and respect the group's diversity. There is a fundamental difference between compromise and flexibility. When we compromise the vision, we make it what it was not intended to be. When we are flexible, we find ways to accomplish the mission. A jet's wings are flexible. This is so the plane may fly through the currents by allowing its wings to bend and not break. An organization will be required to navigate through its share of currents. Flexibility is the key here for success.

Special Notes to Team Members

- The Leader will cast the vision.
- The Leader leads.
- Remember the personal needs of the leader; many leaders will not willingly share their needs.
- Leaders are appointed by God.
- Team members serve the leader and serve with integrity.
- Vision fulfillment is a team effort.
- Remember the wineskin from which you are operating. This determines your role as a team member.
- A Leader must have a covering also.

The Corporate Vision is the truly successful stage. It is no longer the leader or team's vision. It is now *their* vision. Collectively, they all own it and have a growing passion for its success. At this stage the vision is clear, challenging, and attainable. It is a vision complete with a mission and statement, major areas, and well-defined action steps. It is a complete vision that is biblical, future oriented, directional, and functional.

The organization can run with it. The vision produces passion and a high commitment level. This vision will live and develop as the organization lives and develops. Its focus is on the present challenges with an eye toward the future. The fears, hopes, and dreams of the leader, team, partners, and the communities that the organization serves and hopes to serve are considered and accounted for within the framework of the corporate vision. It is important to understand your organizational structure fully. I have been a part of organizations that elected leaders who operated from a different structure than the one they met in place. The ground rules changed almost overnight and resulted in confusion and uncertainty. It is paramount for all stakeholders to be on the same page and know what to expect and what is expected from them. Take quality time with this personal study section; the future successes of your organization may depend on it.

Personal Study

Wine and Wineskins

Session Topic: In this session, you will review your organizational structure and vision-casting methods.

Practical Wisdom Discovery

1. Briefly describe your organizational structure and state which of the two camps it most identifies with.
2. Why is an understanding of wineskin structures important in vision building? Fully explain.
3. What are the three stages of a vision's development? Which one do you see as most difficult?
4. Name your team members and list what gifts each bring to the organization.
5. Why is it important to put new wine into new wineskins? Give at least three reasons.
6. What assistance do you need in establishing your organizational structure? Discuss with your team and develop a plan of action.

Assignment: Write an essay of your first leadership role. List the ups and downs and what you learned from these experiences. Share the information with your core group of leaders as a mentoring session.

Prayer Focus:

- Pray for your leadership team, asking God to clearly define their roles.
- Take time to praise and thank God for the vision He has given you.
- Prayer for your area; ask God to reveal unseen needs and concerns.
- Ask God to help you be more long-suffering with those entrusted to your care.

Pray These Scriptures This Week

Exodus 35:35 Psalm 63:4 Acts 4:24 Romans 5:5

Shifts and Challenges

"He who stops being better stops being good."[13] Oliver Cromwell

In the winter of 2003, I was contracted by a major North American corporation to work with their regional managers. This proved to be interesting and rewarding. The corporation's annual gross revenue, which was in the billions, was sliding, and the corporation was concerned that they were falling behind the competition in a particular division. They had recently shifted their vision statement and were confident that they had the pulse of the targeted market; however, they were losing clients. What was the problem?

This book was written for Christian leaders and their organizations; however, by sharing an illustration of how a major corporation approached their shifts and challenges, I hope to impress upon you the need for critical thinking and analyzing.

Shifts are normal in organizations. A shift is when an organization changes its vision, direction, focus, mission, or goals. There are any numbers of reasons why an organization goes through shifts in its vision, and not all shifts prove to be positive; however, all are repairable over time.

Challenges are a part of the process of change and development for an organization. Often, a challenge will result from a shift. Challenges also influence shifts.

I met with the principal employees of the corporation, and

through dialogue and a specially designed workshop, we made some important discoveries and embarked on a revision process.

The Revision Process

Vision Statement. As I previously stated, the statement was changed. It was changed from a *service* concept to a *partnership* concept. It appeared simple enough, but there were some major challenges:

- The service concept required the regional manager to visit the physical plants in his section and work directly with the plant manager.

- The partnership concept required that a regional manager visit the physical plants in his section and work first with the company's president and then the plant manager.

The focus was now partnering rather than serving. Partnering is a powerful and a marketable concept. The presidents all embraced the vision shift and eagerly awaited the change. They brought into the idea that their supplier was in partnership with them and would forge a meaningful and lasting relationship starting at the top level.

Challenge. The regional managers were not delivering on the vision shift's expectations. The presidents were upset and threatening canceling contracts. What went wrong? Here are some answers:

Job Descriptions. Job descriptions were never adjusted to accommodate the shift; *therefore no mindset shift took place.*

Temperaments. Some regional managers did not have the temperament for the new thrust. They were comfortable working with the plant managers but felt uneasy forging relationships with company presidents.

Training. Regional managers needed training in recognizing the temperament traits of clients so they could maximize the moment. They needed to say the right thing to the right person.

Solution. You would think that the solution would be a simple one. Give them an updated job description and send them to work. We took a different approach. We chose to build a united team of regional managers, allowing their talents, training, and temperaments to complement and support the efforts of the team:

- *Temperament Profiles* were administered. Prior to the workshop, profiles were administered and then given out during the first day of the workshop. It was rewarding to witness the enthusiasm of the participants. They were committed to their jobs and wanted to succeed in this vision shift. The profiles gave them a snapshot of themselves and guidelines for effective communication with their clients.

- *Roles of a Regional Manager.* Instead of giving them updated job descriptions, we created one together. As opposed to calling it a "job description," we developed the "Seven Roles of a Regional Manager." With the team concept in mind, each regional manager's area of expertise was now available to the overall team. Those who would not be able to adjust to performing in the frontline vision shift (meeting with presidents) would still retain a role as a trainer in the corporation. They would train their replacements and other recruits.

The corporation's board and employees committed to the revised job descriptions or roles and soon the relationships with the various clients improved. Today, that corporation has implemented the personality-profiles concept and corporate-vision-building principles in all divisions of their corporation.

A Ministry Example

Here is another example. A ministry planted a local church in a depressed area of a city. The intent was to win that community to the Lord Jesus Christ and establish a vibrant Christian presence. The ministry was able to secure a building for its meetings and quickly began to grow, attracting children and adults. After a few years, the ministry decided to relocate the church in another part of the city and made the decision to bus in the members from the present community. I advised that it would produce a shift in the church's focus over time. Here are some of the possible future challenges I listed for the leadership:

- People would conclude that the church moved because of the state of the community.
- The original target group would feel second class and abandoned.
- People with greater incomes would be needed to sustain the shift.
- Over time, the original target group would fade out completely or become the minority.
- Problems of bitterness and mistrust could develop.

The ministry decided to move forward with the relocation. Over the years, all of the listed challenges were encountered. However, because of their reliance on the Holy Spirit and their willingness for consultation and training, a plan of action was developed, and each challenge was successfully navigated.

A Biblical Example

Challenges produce defining moments for leaders and organizations. How we handle the challenges we face determine the degree of our successes and failures. The Scriptures record many examples of how leaders faced their challenges. One example that presents a series of God-honoring principles is found in 2 Chronicles 20. Jehoshaphat is in the last chapter of his career as king and faces a severe challenge that turns into a national crisis. The kingdom of Judah is enjoying a peaceful independence when suddenly a powerful combination of enemies threatens the independence of the kingdom. Jehoshaphat's response to the imminent invasion is God honoring and time tested. Here is his response, the events surrounding the challenge, and my commentary:

1. *He hears the troubling news and is afraid, but seeks the Lord* (vs. 3, 4). Bad news often produces fear in our hearts because it threatens our way of life. As leaders, we are not immune to troubles; to the contrary, we experience more than our share of them. The king turns to God; he remembered where his wisdom and strength comes from. He declares a national fast. This is important; if the challenge can possibly affect the complete rank and file of the organization, you might want to consider getting everyone involved in addressing the challenge. All stakeholders must come out of their comfort zones. It is a pride issue for a leader not to share the burden with others. Seeking God ought to be the first response of would be and seasoned leaders, and this response is often meant to be corporate. *He acknowledges the Sovereignty of God* (vs. 5, 6). The king openly acknowledges the sovereignty of God in the form of a prayer in the presence of the nation. This has to build corporate confidence. God is greater than any challenge we may face. This was done in the house of the Lord. Remind God, yourself, and those you lead of how powerful God is.

2. *He reminds God and the people of God's Power displayed in the past* (v. 7). God's power displayed is accompanied with a promise. The land was to be theirs forever. The promise itself is a rallying point. If God gives us an inheritance, is it not safe to conclude that the challenges associated with our blessing are solvable? The king cries to the faithful God of his promise.
3. *He acknowledges the uniqueness of the challenge* (vs. 10-13):
4. When the challenge was humanly manageable, God would not let him address it.
5. He now looks toward God for an answer to the developed challenge.
6. All were stakeholders in the promise; therefore all stood before the Lord.
7. Efficient leaders will address upcoming or perceived challenges; however, there are times when the Lord will not allow leaders to focus on them. In hindsight, the king might have destroyed the enemy when they were not a powerful force, but he was obeying the Lord. Our strategies for our organizations are subject to the will of the Lord. It is important to be sensitive to the leadings of the Holy Spirit. All things do work together for the good of those that Love the Lord (See Romans 8:28).
8. *He was open to Prophesy* (vs.14-17). There was a "Thus saith the Lord unto you." This is the highest form of prophecy. How do you question a "Thus saith the Lord unto you"? It is interesting to note that the writer of the text includes the genealogy of the young prophet. Perhaps this was to establish his credibility by pointing out his family tree for reference, or it simply was to properly identify him for history's sake. What is certain is that he was known. It is vital to test and try the spirit. Know those whom you allow to speak into your life and the life of your organization, especially if they wish to give you a "Thus saith the Lord unto you."

9. There are many false prophets roaming throughout the Body of Christ, confusing and destroying lives with their enticing words. Leaders in desperation or ignorance may be deceived and thrown off track. God will at times give you a "Thus saith the Lord unto you"; however, I have often found that the form of prophesy normally received is "For it seemed good to the Holy Ghost, and to us, to lay upon you no greater burden than these necessary things" (Acts 15:28). This implies that after seeking the Lord concerning the matter and searching our own hearts, we believe this is God's will for the matter. We may not be one hundred percent right, but we might be.
10. A "Thus saith the Lord unto you" declares there is no room for error. Make sure the prophet is not in error. How can you be sure of this? The prophecy must be biblically based and must bear witness in your spirit by resulting in a spirit of peace. Your spirit must bear witness. God gave His solution to their challenge and it included His abiding power and presence.
11. *He led the people in worship and praise of God* (vs. 18, 19). It is the duty of the soul to worship and praise God. It is also a telltale sign of faith. Can you worship and praise God based solely on His Word and past performances? Can you worship and praise the Lord in the face of your challenges? The soul's past, present, and future are hidden in Him when we continually worship and praise Him. The Scripture declares that God dwells among the praises of His people (See Psalms 2:3). Wherever He dwells, He has a vested interest. Worship and praise in the midst of your challenges crushes the spirit of fear and releases the anointing of the Holy Spirit.
12. *He and the people planned their Strategy* (vs. 20-22). God gave the strategy for the non-battle; they planned their strategy for praise:

13. They rose early. Respond immediately to God's timing. All great leaders respond to God's timing. Abraham rose early to offer his son. Joshua rose early to cross his Jordan. Jesus rose early to pray and rose early from the grave in victory.
14. They were told to believe God so they may be established. Belief in God is necessary for sustained success. It is our belief in God that establishes us and the vision of our organizations.
15. They were told to believe His prophets so they may prosper. When a prophetic word is uttered by one of God's prophets, it is often conditional in that the full effect is realized when we believe and follow the instructions given. If the king and his subjects did not believe and participate in their assigned roles, they surely would not have been in place to gather the spoils. The king and his kingdom followed God's action steps for the plan and the victory was secured. It is recorded that the challenge (invading armies) made the nation richer and more powerful. It took the king and his people three days to collect the spoils of war. Perhaps this is why God would not allow the king to crush the nations when they were less developed. Smaller nations would have provided fewer spoils. Often, your blessings are wrapped up in your challenges; this is why it is essential for leaders to obey the voice of the Holy Spirit in all matters of the soul and leadership. God is not a novice; He is the instructor and we are the apprentices. Trust Him and learn from Him; this will provide you with future confidence in the face of challenges.

Shifts and challenges can prove rewarding for your organization. Change is growth, and growth produces change. In our workshops on *Building Your Vision*, the *Practical Wisdom* principles shared in this book are expounded upon.

Personal Study

Shifts and Challenges

Session Topic: In this session, you will review shifts and challenges.

Practical Wisdom Discovery

1. List at least three challenges that your organization is facing.
2. Explain what a shift is.
3. List a shift in your organization, and fully explain why you think it may have occurred.
4. In what way can a shift be positive?
5. Can you name a negative shift that your organization encountered? And if so, what was it?
6. What concerns you the most about you're pending challenges?

Assignment: List an organizational shift and then work with a team to design possible solutions for that shift.

Prayer Focus:

- Pray for guidance in your shifts.

- Take time to praise and thank God for the vision He has given you.
- Commit to walk in obedience in all areas of your life.
- Ask God to help you be future focused.

Pray These Scriptures This Week

Zechariah 10:6, 12 Psalm 74:20 Romans 11:11 Ephesians 1:18

Conclusion

> "There is a time to be born, and a time to die, says Solomon, and it is the memento of a truly wise man; but there is an interval between these two times of infinite importance." [14] Leigh Richmond

Now that you have read the book and hopefully have completed the personal study sections, you may be asking, "Where from here?" *The 5RCircle Process* Workbook included in your book is formatted to take you and your team through the complete steps to *Building Your Vision*. The workbook is interactive in nature, and its objectives are as follows:

1. To help you see the importance of and a commitment to the development of a *Complete Vision* for your organization.
2. To present to you and your team the various *Building Blocks* of a *Complete Vision* for your organization.
3. To provide a format for your team to use the building blocks in the development or revision of your *Complete Vision*.

Guidelines

The material in the workbook was originally developed for *Building Your Vision* workshops and was field tested for three years. Here are two options for how the workbook may be used:

1. You may wish to gather your core leaders and spend a weekend developing your vision using the 5*RCircle Process* Workbook. The *Practical Wisdom Team* is available to serve as your facilitator.
2. You may wish to use the workbook in a weekly group setting and develop your vision over a prolonged period of time.

I highly recommend that you have some form of interaction with our Practical Wisdom Team. We also tailor workshops and seminars to meet the needs of our clients and offer additional consulting and training services.

THE CTC NETWORK
Suite #31 Pioneer's Professional Plaza
P.O. Box F-43455
Freeport, Bahamas
TEL: (242) 351-7035 or (242) 349-1137
www.ctcnetwork.org

Building Your Vision
The 5RCircle Process

Introduction

The following workbook has been provided to give you a working tool for building your vision. It was developed over a three year field-testing exercise and has proven worthwhile and effective for various organizations and ministries. The objectives of the workbook are as follows:

- To help you see the importance of and a commitment to the development of a *Complete Vision* for your organization or ministry.
- To present the various building blocks of a C*omplete Vision*.
- To provide a format for your team to use the building blocks in the development or revision of your *Complete Vision*.

The principles and methods presented in this workbook may also be used in personal vision planning. They are designed in a format that allows easy adaptation to almost any vision-building endeavor. Let's begin the process!

Practical Wisdom Points for Your Vision Statement

Possible Components: Areas to consider in writing your Vision Statement. Think about your current vision and use some of these components to express in writing your current vision. Please check which ones apply.

Lost Society (Gather and Grow)

- The Great Commission Mandate

  ____

- Un-churched

  ____

- Special Target

  ____

Saved Society (Gather, Maintain, and Grow)

- Members

  ____

- Possible members

  ____

- Personnel

  ____

- Extended Body of Christ (Local and Global)

  ____

- Leadership

____

Facilities (Obtain, Maintain, and Grow)

- Temporary

____

- Permanent

____

- Missions/Facilities in other countries

____

- Camps

____

- Schools

____

Products and Services (Develop, Maintain, and Grow)

- What you do

____

- What you offer

____

- What you make

____

- What you sell

  ____

- What you distribute

  ____

- What you provide

  ____

List your components from the list provided, plus any others you might have. Arrange them in the provided *categories*, and place them in your *priority* order.

1 ______________________________

2 ______________________________

3 ______________________________

4 ______________________________

5 ______________________________

6 ______________________________

7 ______________________________

Now that you have completed this step, construct a complete sentence for each component and link the sentences together. Use the next page for this exercise.

YOUR CURRENT VISION STATEMENT

As you begin this process of writing or rewriting your vision, I ask that you use the format provided and write your current vision statement. If you do not have a vision statement as yet, write the general idea of what you do as an organization.

Your Current Vision Statement

Category

____

____

____

____

Category

____

____

____

____

Category

____

____

____

____

Category

____

____

____

____

Practical Wisdom Points

What is presently the driving force behind your organization/ministry? Possible Components: Which one(s) reflects your organization or ministry? Some of these components are negative in nature. They are listed for the sole purpose of exposing hidden motivators. Carefully and prayerfully evaluate your organization or ministry and as a group discuss your findings.

The Driving Force: Are You?

- Personality Driven

  ____

- Relationship Driven

  ____

- Missions Driven

  ____

- Time Line Driven

  ____

- Need Driven

  ____

- Program Driven

  ____

- Purpose Driven

  ____

- Product Driven

  ____

- Results Driven

  ____

- Procedure Driven

  ____

- People Driven

  ____

- Power Driven

  ____

- Ethnicity Driven

  ____

- Prophecy Driven

  ____

- Tradition Driven

  ____

- Pride Driven

  ____

- Perspective Driven

  ____

- Vision Driven

  ____

- Cause Driven

  ____

- ______________________________ Driven

Discussion Questions

We are ________________ driven.

We believe we are this way because

Are you satisfied with your present driving force? Please explain.

List two advantages of your driving force:

List a disadvantage of your driving force:

Notes

Vision

It is important to be able to write your vision. A written vision is a biblical principle. It is our prayer that you will allow the Holy Spirit to *guide* you in this process. It is critical that you remain committed to the writing exercise. As you progress with the exercises, you will see your corporate vision take shape and become well defined.

By staying committed, you and your team will identify the way forward for your organization. You will also uncover challenges preventing success and develop solutions for these challenges as a team.

You have just completed writing your current vision statement or what you do as an organization and have listed and discussed your driving force. Now, from what you presently do and from what you have gleaned by reading, prayer, and discussion, write what you envision your organization becoming.

What Kind of Organization Would You Like To Become?

Think for a moment and write the answer in one complete sentence.

____

____

____

____

____

Throughout this workbook, you ought to interpret the reference to vision as a vision complete with a mission statement, major areas of focus, and well-defined action steps. A complete vision is biblical, future oriented, directional, and functional.

Practical Wisdom Points:

- A Vision produces a mission; if not it remains a dream.
- Various divisions of an organization or ministry may have a Vision. You may wish to call them Sub-Visions.
- A Vision is future oriented; however, once reached, then what? You must always be planning ahead.
- Remember that flexibility is imperative for success in this process. You will want to continually draw from the insights and perspectives of your group.

Our Developmental Process of a Vision

Here is the developmental process that will be used in building your vision:

- *Recap* your history
- *Recognize* your shifts in Vision
- *Rework* your challenges
- *Rewrite* your Vision
- *Redesign* your hinge statements

The process is designed to be continuous in nature. This five-fold developmental process ought to be completed on a regular basis. A complete vision evolves as an organization or ministry grows. We call this process *The 5RCircle Process.*

The 5RCircle Process

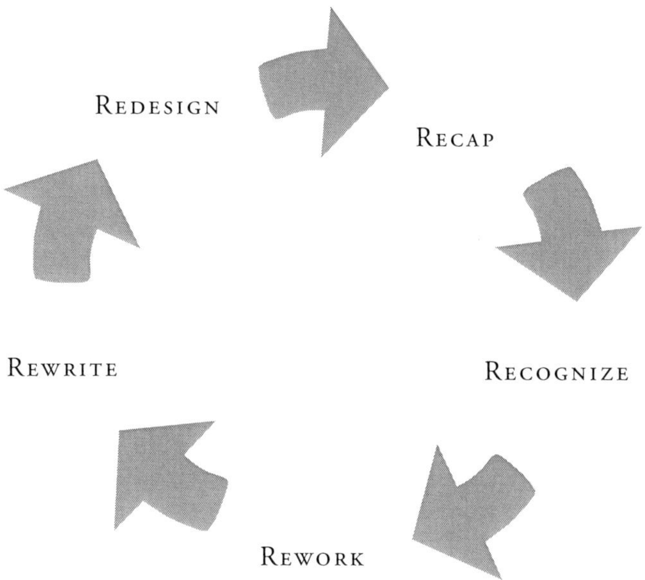

Recap History

"Concept of History, history as commonly understood, may refer to events themselves or the record of events. The Greek word for history originally meant investigation or research. In time, the word came to refer to the written account, summary, of the results of research."[15]

Let's define "history" as *His-Story*, the events of a person or organization's life. When we can recap and identify with the past, it helps us to understand the developmental process that is taking place. This recapping helps identify trends in our organization as well as trends in our communities. Often, there appears to be a circle effect to our history. By documentation, we are better able to recognize this ever-widening circle and understand and be in position to articulate its importance.

Our history continues to grow day by day and event by event and is a determining factor in our decisions. Often, the fruit of the future of your organization is contained in the seed or seeds of its past. Having your past up-to-date so to speak will allow you and your team to educate new workers and partners and have readily available useful information for planning.

As you complete this exercise, pay special attention to the original purpose of the organization for the period of time in which it was created. *Why was this organization or ministry necessary? Is its purpose still valid today?* Keep these two valid questions in focus; they assist in determining what shifts, if any, the organization has or needs to make. Also, an understanding of an organization's history will be of great benefit to new leaders or members in that it helps prevent misunderstandings by producing a clear picture.

An updated history helps all to understand and appreciate the foundation from which the organization or ministry is functioning. If a new wine or wineskin shift took place, there might be lingering factors or peculiarities that require tactfulness. Often, new leadership is unaware of the caterpillar-like struggles that an organization has endured. The caterpillar is engrained in the butterfly and must be accounted for. The complete story does not have to be made common knowledge, but it ought to be documented and shared on a need-to-know basis. Recapping preserves proper protocol.

Here's an example of how knowledge of an organization's past would have benefited a new leader in a rural setting.

Practical Wisdom Point:

Sometime back, I visited with a retired minister who appeared very bitter. As I listened to *His-Story*, it became obvious that his root of bitterness stemmed from seeing a part of his life's work neglected. He was living close to a church facility that he helped build, and in his opinion, the facility was always in a poor state. He was watching a significant part of his past destroyed in front of his eyes. This, coupled with the retirement stage, or season of his life, was adversely affecting his health.

This retired minister often attempted to reach out to the new, younger minister but was rejected. Eventually, the influence that the retired minister enjoyed in the community was used in a negative fashion and undermined the work of the young minister and the local church.

Adequate knowledge of the ministry's history would have assisted the present minister in understanding this relationship challenge. The present minister had no clue that the retired minister was instrumental in the development of the local church he was leading. He assumed that the retired minister was just meddling in the local church's business. A documented history and its most recent recap would have been most beneficial in this instance.

When our sons were young, they loved to watch cartoons early on Saturday mornings. Their favorite by far was "G.I. Joe." The tag line for this cartoon series was: "Knowing is half the battle." This is the intention of the recapping of your organization's history. It provides *knowledge* so that you may apply *Practical Wisdom* principles. Hosea 4:6 declares:

> "My people are destroyed for lack of knowledge." Here is what Jesus said in respect to being wise: "And the lord commended the unjust steward, because he had done wisely: for the children of this world are in their generation wiser than the children of light" (Luke 16:8).

An accurate knowledge of the history of an organization can keep everything in proper perspective.

Recap Questions

Who was the principal person and/or group that started the organization?

What type of organization was it when first launched? (Church, Para-Church, Missions, etc.)

What fellowship, if any, was it a part of?

Does it still hold the same status today? If not, what status does it have?

When was the organization started? Date and Time

What was Special about that period of time?

Where was the organization started? *What* city, town, or settlement?

What type of facility?

Why was the organization started?

How did the organization develop? Please list major points, starting from its formation to its present position (name or location change, revivals, church plants, various leaders, etc).

Date

Date

Date

Date

Date

Date

Date

Date

Date

Date

Recognize Shifts

Shifts in vision are normal for organizations. A shift is when an organization or ministry changes its direction, focus, mission, or goals.

There is any number of reasons why an organization experiences shifts in its vision. Some shifts prove to be positive, while others are recognized as negative; however, negative shifts are repairable over time. The recognition of shifts is part of your vision-evaluation process and often is in your major area, even though it might, at times, be in the core structure of your vision statement. A shift is a major indicator that there are areas of the vision that are not working properly or have expanded and are not accounted for. After proper evaluation, you will be in a position to make the necessary adjustments.

This recognition exercise will allow you and your team to recognize your shifts and the reason(s) for them and allow you to document their results. This may all prove very rewarding for your organization in that it gives you a snapshot of the changes taking place within the framework of your organization and the communities which it serves. As a team, you may be more readily able to make the necessary adjustments where needed and collectively decide on a positive approach for articulating the shifts to the rank and file of the organization or ministry.

Practical Wisdom Points:

- The Bible contains examples of shifts in vision. (Jesus' mission is one case in point. He came to the Jew first and was rejected.)
- History contains examples of shifts in vision (from automobile corporations to educational institutions).
- In our Personal Lives we have all experienced shifts in vision.

Here is a list of possible reasons why an organization may have experienced a shift. This partial list may assist you in identifying the reasons for your shifts.

Shifts:

- Internal Growth Patterns

  ____

- Community Growth Patterns

  ____

- Improved Product

  ____

- Improved Services

  ____

- Technology

  ____

- Knowledge Enhancement

  ____

- Acquisitions

  ____

- Merger

  ____

- Vision Realization

  ____

- Leadership Changes

  ____

- Personal or Organizational Failure

  ____

- Natural Disasters

  ____

- Loss of Facilities

  ____

- Economic Challenges

  ____

- Change of Location

  ____

- Change of Doctrine

  ____

- External Growth Patterns

  ____

- Change of Covering

  ____

- Personnel Challenges

  ____

- Other

  ____

  ____

Brainstorm with your team and identify your shifts. Document your findings. Remember, the above list contains some reasons (challenges) that might have produced a shift. In the process that follows, you will want to identify shifts that have or are taking place. Recognizing and documenting how you have changed your direction, focus, mission, or goals is the goal of this exercise.

Notes

Recognize Questions

Shift One

List the shift: (What Changed?)

Answer why the shift occurred: (What caused the shift?)

State the results of the shift:

Positive:

1.

2.

3.

Negative:

1.

2.

3.

Recognize Questions

Shift Two

List the shift:

Answer why the shift occurred:

State the results of the shift:

Positive:

1.

2.

3.

4.

Negative:

1.

2.

3.

Recognize Questions

Shift Three

List the shift:

Answer why the shift occurred:

State the results of the shift:

Positive:

1.

2

3.

Negative:

1.

2.

3.

Rework Challenges

Challenges are a part of the process of change and development for an organization or ministry. Challenges will produce shifts and often are the results of shifts. Vision is often future focused, but its mission and major areas are typically present focused. If we can adequately address the challenges, we can accomplish the mission and ultimately fulfill the vision. Challenges in themselves become a working part of the mission process and actions steps of the vision. Like your shifts, reworking your challenges is a part of your evaluation and adjustment processes. This process of reworking your challenges has three steps:

- *List* the top six challenges. We recommend that you only list the top six because many challenges are interrelated. Listing only six will force you and your team to look for the core, or root, challenges and not the off-shoots. This step allows the team to agree on what is affecting the vision's fulfillment. Do not rush this process.

- *Link* them if possible to the current vision or mission statement. Some challenges can be linked to the current vision statement. If the current vision statement and its major areas of focus can accommodate the challenges, you may continue on your current course. However, we have found that many challenges will result in an organization or ministry having to alter its overall vision. Make a note of the challenges that do not link.

- *Line* the challenges that do not link to the revised vision. Line challenges that do not link indicate that the vision or mission statement is in the process of revision. *Please note that when you rewrite your complete vision, you must take in account these challenges that do not link to your present vision or mission statements. They must be accounted for in the revised vision. They are often accounted for in the major areas and action steps of the complete vision.*

Practical Wisdom Points:

- Challenges are normal for organizations and ministries.
- Challenges are positive in that they confirm growth patterns.
- Challenges are positive in that they confirm negative trends.
- Challenges provide opportunities for new leaders to emerge.
- Challenges may be personnel, facility, system, or financial in nature.
- Challenges are both man created and nature produced.
- Challenges are stepping stones toward success.
- Challenges may produce vision shifts.
- Challenges are often the result of vision shifts.
- Challenges may result from right choices.
- Challenges may result from wrong decisions.
- Challenges have a mind of their own.
- Challenges may be road blocks or road signs.
- Challenges can be conquered.
- Challenges provide opportunities for trust in God.

Rework Questions

Challenge One

The L.A.S Process

List the Challenge:

Answer why the Challenge occurred:

State the results of the Challenge:

1.

2.

3.

Possible Solutions:

1.

2.

3.

Can This Challenge Be Linked To Your Current Vision?

Yes

No

Rework Questions

Challenge Two

List the Challenge:

Answer why the Challenge occurred:

State the results of the Challenge:

1.

2.

3.

Possible Solutions:

1.

2.

3.

Can This Challenge Be Linked To Your Current Vision?

Yes

No

Rework Questions

Challenge Three

List the Challenge:

Answer why the Challenge occurred:

State the results of the Challenge:

1.

2.

3.

Possible Solutions:

1.

2.

3. ____

____

____

____

Can This Challenge Be Linked To Your Current Vision?

Yes ____

No ____

Rework Questions

Challenge Four

List the Challenge:

____

____

____

____

____

Answer why the Challenge occurred:

____

____

____

____

____

State the results of the Challenge:

1.

2.

3.

Possible Solutions:

1.

2.

3. ______

______

______

______

Can This Challenge Be Linked To Your Current Vision?

Yes ______

No ______

Rework Questions

Challenge Five

List the Challenge:

______

______

______

______

______

Answer why the Challenge occurred:

______

______

______

______

______

State the results of the Challenge:

1.

2.

3.

Possible Solutions:

1.

2.

3.

Can This Challenge Be Linked To Your Current Vision?

Yes

No

Rework Questions

Challenge Six

List the Challenge:

Answer why the Challenge occurred:

State the results of the Challenge:

1.

2.

3.

Possible Solutions:

1.

2.

3.

Can This Challenge Be Linked To Your Current Vision?

Yes

No

Building Your Vision-Flow Chart

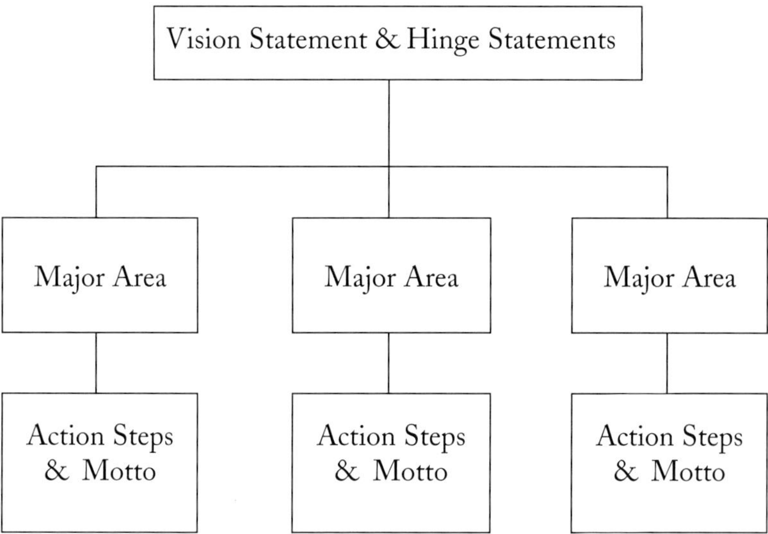

You are now ready to write or rewrite your vision. The writing or rewriting of your vision will involve a four-step process:

- *Define* your Vision. This is the stating or restating of your vision statement. You will review your current vision statement, desired vision statement, shifts, and challenges, and then readjust your vision statement as necessary.
- *Design* your major areas. You may wish to identify at least five

major areas. These areas will pertain to the mission part of the vision and must take into account your shifts and challenges. Major areas may be developmental, maintenance, and growth related. Major areas may focus on people, places, programs, procedures, and products.

- *Develop* your action steps. You will develop a set for each major area. These are the steps to be taken to realize the goals of the major areas. Action steps may be the appointment of personnel that will be charged with the actual developing of action steps, or it may be the designing of the actions steps by your leadership team. You may wish to be creative and develop your action steps by combining the two approaches.
- *Declare* your motto for each major area. This should be a brief statement expressing the goal of the major area. Mottos ought to be catchy and may be used in a variety of ways (bumper stickers, decals, etc.).

Please note that the hinge statements are designed last, because they express in a condensed form the complete vision.

Define Your Vision

- *Define* your Vision. This is the stating or restating of your vision statement. You will review your current vision statement, desired vision statement, shifts, and challenges, and then readjust your vision statement as necessary.

Vision Statement:

Major Area—One

- *Design your major areas.* You may wish to identify at least five major areas. These areas will pertain to the mission part of the vision and must take into account your shifts and challenges. Major areas may be developmental, maintenance, and growth related. Major areas may focus on people, places, programs, procedures, and products.

Design Major Area of Focus:

Team Leader:

He/She reports to:

Team Members:

1.

2.

3.

4.

5.

6.

7.

Major Area One—Action Steps

- *Develop* your action steps. You will develop a set for each major area. These are the steps to be taken to realize the goals of the major areas. Action steps may be the appointment of personnel that will be charged with the actual developing of action steps, or it may be the designing of the actions steps by your leadership team. You may wish to be creative and develop your action steps by combining the two approaches.

Make sure your action steps have time lines.

1.

2.

3.

4.

5.

Declare Your One—Sentence Motto

Declare your motto for each major area. This should be a brief statement expressing the goal of the major area. Mottos ought to be catchy and may be used in a variety of ways (bumper stickers, decals, etc.).

Major Area—Two

Design Major Area of Focus:

Team Leader:

He/She reports to:

Team Members:

1.

2.

3.

4.

5.

6.

7.

Major Area Two—Action Steps

1.

2.

3.

4.

5.

Declare Your Two—Sentence Motto

Declare your motto for each major area. This should be a brief statement expressing the goal of the major area. Mottos ought to be catchy and may be used in a variety of ways (bumper stickers, decals, etc.).

Major Area—Three

Design Major Area of Focus:

Team Leader:

He/She reports to:

Team Members:

1.

2.

3.

4.

5.

6.
7.

Major Area Three—Action Steps

1.
2.
3.
4.
5.

Declare Your Three—Sentence Motto

Declare your motto for each major area. This should be a brief statement expressing the goal of the major area. Mottos ought to be catchy and may be used in a variety of ways (bumper stickers, decals, etc.).

Major Area—Four

Design Major Area of Focus:

____

____

____

____

____

____

____

____

____

____

Team Leader: _______________

He/She reports to: _______________

Team Members: _______________

1. _______________

2. _______________

3. _______________

4. _______________

5. _______________

6.

7.

Major Area Four—Action Steps

1.

2.

3.

4.

5.

Declare Your Four—Sentence Motto

Declare your motto for each major area. This should be a brief statement expressing the goal of the major area. Mottos ought to be catchy and may be used in a variety of ways (bumper stickers, decals, etc.).

Major Area—Five

Design Major Area of Focus:

Team Leader:

He/She reports to:

Team Members:

1.

2.

3.

4.

5.

6. ____

7. ____

Major Area Five—Action Steps

1. ____

2. ____

3. ____

4. ____

5. ____

Declare Your Five—Sentence Motto

Declare your motto for each major area. This should be a brief statement expressing the goal of the major area. Mottos ought to be catchy and may be used in a variety of ways (bumper stickers, decals, etc.).

MAJOR AREA—SIX

DESIGN MAJOR AREA OF FOCUS:

Team Leader:

He/She reports to:

Team Members:

1.

2.

3.

4.

5.

6.

7.

Major Area Six—Action Steps

1.

2.

3.

4.

5.

Declare Your Six—Sentence Motto

Declare your motto for each major area. This should be a brief statement expressing the goal of the major area. Mottos ought to be catchy and may be used in a variety of ways (bumper stickers, decals, etc.).

Major Area—Seven

Design Major Area of Focus:

Team Leader:

He/She reports to:

Team Members:

1.

2.

3.

4.

5.

6. ______________________________

7. ______________________________

Major Area Seven—Action Steps

1. ______________________________

2. ______________________________

3. ______________________________

4. ______________________________

5. ______________________________

Declare Your Seven—Sentence Motto

Declare your motto for each major area. This should be a brief statement expressing the goal of the major area. Mottos ought to be catchy and may be used in a variety of ways (bumper stickers, decals, etc.).

____

____

____

____

Redesign Hinge Statements

Hinge Statements are important because they allow us and others to see the principles that hold our vision together. This exercise, when carried out properly, is valuable in that it reminds us that our vision must be sensitive to the needs of both the Lost and Saved Societies as well as the needs of our facilities.

Our statements become the hinges that hold the vision upright and allow for its movement and access. Core values are more easily derived from clear hinge statements.

Practical Wisdom Points:

- Hinge statements are maintenance and growth related.
- Hinge statements may be displayed for all to see.
- Hinge statements focus on people, products, and places.
- Hinge statements are conversation starters.
- Hinge statements are visible reminders.

Sample: *The CTC Network* (Client-related hinge statements)

- To collaborate with our clients to reach innovative solutions to their present challenges.
- To assist our clients in developing action plans to ensure continued success.

Hinge Statements

Condense your vision statement and major areas into hinge statements. This is accomplished by looking over your vision statement, major areas, and motto statements, and then writing a brief statement that represents their core purposes.

People:

Maintenance Statement:

Growth Statement:

People:

Maintenance Statement:

Growth Statement:

Places:

Maintenance Statement:

Growth Statement:

Places:

Maintenance Statement:

Growth Statement:

Product:

Maintenance Statement:

Growth Statement:

Product:

Maintenance Statement:

Growth Statement:

You may wish to compile the developed vision in pamphlet form and circulate it among the members of your organization and target groups. Please remember that this 5*RCircle Process/Building Your Vision* process may and ought to be repeated whenever it is deemed necessary.

The process of success is often a widening circle, and its expansion is the direct result of the leader not only embracing the purposes of God, but the reality of needed change. *God Bless!*

THE CTC NETWORK
Suite #31 Pioneer's Professional Plaza
P.O. Box F-43455
Freeport, Bahamas
TEL: (242) 351-7035 or (242) 349-1137
www.ctcnetwork.org

Endnotes

1. Thinkexist.com- 2007
2. Nash, Johnny. *I Can See Clearly Now*. Epic Records: 1972.
3. Mead, Frank S. 12,000 *Religious Quotations.* Grand Rapids, Michigan: Baker Book House, 1989. pg. 465
4. Vine, W.E. *Vines Expository Dictionary of Old and New Testament Words*. Iowa Falls, Iowa: World Bible Publishers, 1981. pg. 311
5. Vine, W.E. *Vines Expository Dictionary of Old and New Testament Words*. Iowa Falls, Iowa: World Bible Publishers, 1981. pg. 298
6. *Webster Comprehensive Dictionary*. Chicago: J.G. Ferguson Publishing Company, 1988. pg. 1388
7. Cabinet Office Ref: C.579, *Letter of Appointment.* Nassau, Bahamas: The 28th of May, 1998
8. Mead, Frank S. 12,000 *Religious Quotations.* Grand Rapids, Michigan: Baker Book House, 1989. pg. 341
9. Mead, Frank S. 12,000 *Religious Quotations.* Grand Rapids, Michigan: Baker Book House, 1989. pg. 138

10. Vine, W.E. *Vines Expository Dictionary of Old and New Testament Words*. Iowa Falls, Iowa: World Bible Publishers, 1981. pg. 208

11. Mead, Frank S. 12,000 *Religious Quotations.* Grand Rapids, Michigan: Baker Book House, 1989. pg. 455

12. C. Peter Wagner. *Changing Church*. Ventura, California: Regal Books, 2004. pg. 34

13. Mead, Frank S. 12,000 *Religious Quotations.* Grand Rapids, Michigan: Baker Book House, 1989. pg. 328

14. Mead, Frank S. 12,000 *Religious Quotations.* Grand Rapids, Michigan: Baker Book House, 1989. pg. 444

15. Collier's Encyclopedia, Volume 12. Macmillan Educational Company: 1983. pg. 149

Bibliography

1. Arno, Richard & Phyllis. Creation Therapy. Sarasota, Florida.: Sarasota Academy of Christian Counseling, 1993
2. Elmer, Duane. Cross Cultural Conflict. Downers Grove, Illinois: Inter Varsity Press, 1993
3. Sheets, Dutch. Intercessory Prayer. Venture, California: Regal Books, 1996
4. Shibley, David. A Force in the Earth. Lake Mary, Florida: Charisma House, 1997
5. Vine, W.E. Vines Expository Dictionary of Old and New Testament Words Iowa Falls, Iowa: World Bible Publishers, 1981
6. Wagner, C. Peter. Changing Church. Ventura, California: Regal Books, 2004